STUART McHARDY is a writer, occasional broadcaster, and storyteller. Having been actively involved in many aspects of Scottish culture throughout his adult life – music, poetry, language, history, folklore – he has been resident in Edinburgh for over a quarter of a century. Although he has held some illustrious positions including Director of the Scots Language Resource Centre in Perth and President of the Pictish Arts Society, McHardy is probably proudest of having been a member of the Vigil for a Scottish Parliament. Often to be found in the bookshops, libraries and tea-rooms of Edinburgh, he lives near the city centre with the lovely (and ever-tolerant) Sandra and they have one son, Roderick.

DONALD SMITH is Director of the Scottish Storytelling Centre at Edinburgh's Netherbow and a founder of the National Theatre of Scotland. For many years he was responsible for the programme of the Netherbow Theatre, producing, directing, adapting and writing professional theatre and community dramas, as well as a stream of literature and storytelling events. He has published both poetry and prose and is a founding member of Edinburgh's Guid Crack Club. He also arranges story walks around Arthur's Seat.

Arthur's Seat

Journeys and Evocations

Stuart McHardy and Donald Smith

Luath Press Ltd
Edinburgh

www.luath.co.uk

First published 2012

ISBN: 978-1-908373-46-5

The paper used in this book is sourced from
renewable forestry and is FSC credited material

The paper used in this book is recyclable.
It is made from low-chlorine pulps
produced in a low-energy, low-emissions
manner from renewable forests.

Printed and bound by
TJ International Ltd., Padstow

Typeset in 10.5pt Sabon by
3btype.com

Contents

Introduction

From whatever direction you approach Arthur's Seat you gain a different perspective. No two viewpoints are alike. This is partly because the hill called Arthur's Seat is itself part of a triple peak, set within a wider system of ridges, crags and valleys which slope in long overlapping lines from the main summit towards the Firth of Forth. The geologists describe this as a Crag and Tail, formed through volcanic activity succeeded by glaciers and erosion.

While these may be the physical causes of what we see, their effect is a complex visual artwork that can be viewed in the round; landscape, painting and sculpture is on exhibit in 360 degrees. Added to this are ever changing perspectives of imagery in motion, sometimes in sunlight, sometimes through shifting mists, sometimes veiled by driving rain, and occasionally mantled by eerie white snow. By night the hill may be no more than a dark shadow, or it may be luminous in moonlight, or wanly lit by distant stars.

Ritual fires and signal beacons have blazed on the hill through millennia, while recently maliciously fired whin-bushes have snaked red burns through the black. But the present mood is more subdued; in 2012 Arthur's Seat becomes a remarkable platform for nva's Speed of Light, a fusion of innovative public art and sporting endeavour. The runners of the Speed of Light project have borne glowing light packs to weave subtle patterns of illumination generated by their own movement. Forming part of the 2012 Edinburgh International Festival, Speed of Light is a new visual interpretation of the Hill fuelled by the energy of the 2,000 runners. In this way, Art itself becomes layered and underlayed with nature's own arts.

Angus Farquhar, Creative Director of Speed of Light, has dreamt of creating a work for this particular location for over 20 years.

'I have wanted to create a work on Arthur's Seat since I moved back to Scotland in 1989, so it has occupied a special place in my imagination. Living in London for ten years, I travelled back north for holidays, work and to visit family and realised that I was being emotionally affected by the change in landscape and that particularly higher ground seemed to lead to a rise in feelings of empathy and belonging to that place. I grew up in Edinburgh and to almost all people who have lived there for some time; the mountain has a special place in their hearts or minds.'

The Speed of Light programme extends across seven of Edinburgh's key festivals resulting in newly commissioned works, programmes of discussion, lectures and workshops investigating human endurance, and the relationship of movement to landscape.

Preparations for Speed of Light have involved story-filled walks hosted by the Scottish International Storytelling Festival, and glimpses of Speed of Light, and its place in the unfolding landscape, will be captured within *Arthur's Seat: Journeys and Evocations*. At the moment of the project's realisation, this timely publication draws our close attention to the site itself, and through the form of the walk, follows the pathways of the hill, illuminating the wealth of histories, literature, myths and folklore embedded within Arthur's Seat and its environs.

In this book you can follow a series of journeys through stories, folklore and poetry. Each shed their own kind of illumination on Arthur's Seat, and gives you space to form your personal impressions and experiences of this rich living landscape.

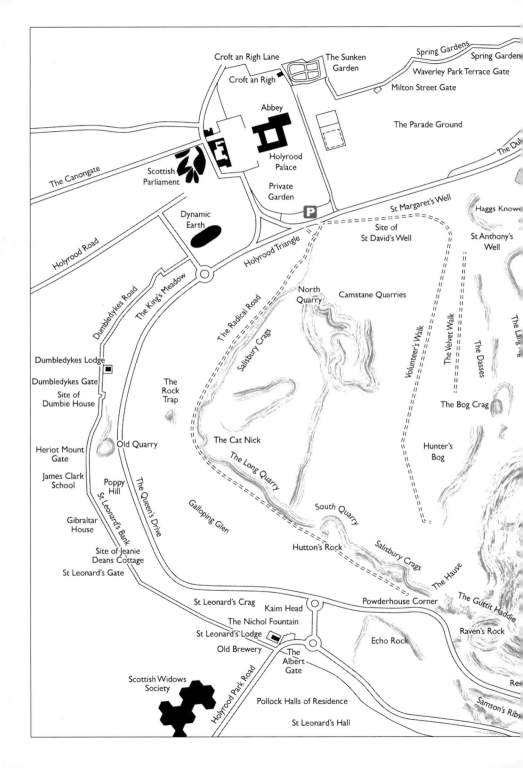

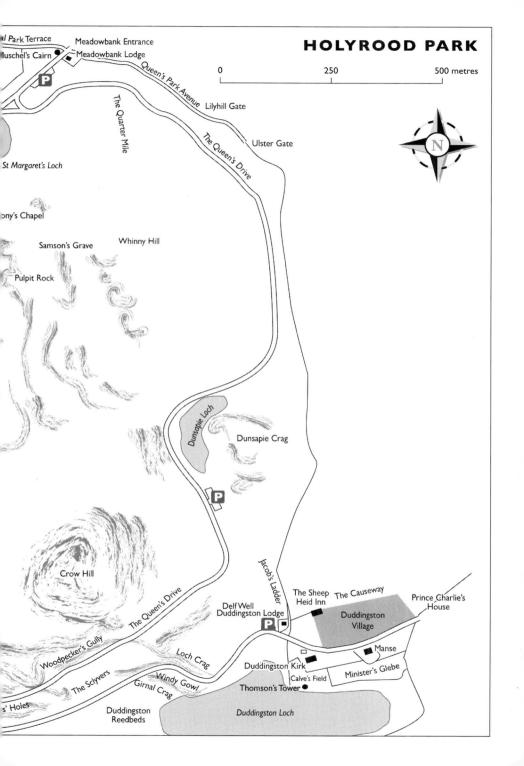

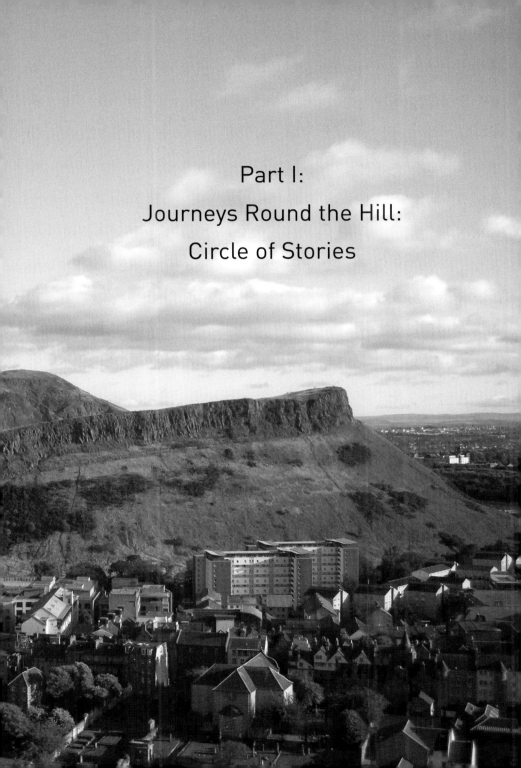

Part I:

Journeys Round the Hill:

Circle of Stories

Holyrood Gateway

There are many gateways into the royal park which surrounds Arthur's Seat, but the best approach is by Holyrood. At the foot of Edinburgh's Royal Mile, the ruins of Holyrood Abbey sit beside and within the Palace of Holyroodhouse. More recently, the spectacular Scottish Parliament designed by Enrico Miralles has been added to the Holyrood configuration.

The common factor is the way each of these successive iconic buildings relates to the park. The Abbey still longs for peace and seclusion; the Palace hugs its enclosure in the same way that royal prerogative once shut off the whole park as a game reserve for their Majesties' pleasure; the Parliament building is the one that reaches out towards the natural contours of the park with landscaped intention. This echoes the way in which the Palace gardens once extended beyond formal enclosures into orchards and vegetable beds, and, finally, the King's Meadow.

These expansive plantings were the creation of Marie de Guise and her daughter Mary Queen of Scots, who emulated and perhaps surpassed the royal French gardens of the Loire at Chenonceau or Blois. The level ground beyond the present palace wall is a reminder of this intermediate realm between wild nature and the institutions of church or state. In recent times this space has been used as a parade ground or tented village for major public events. Enrico Miralles' parliament design explicitly links government and landscape. In Scotland, everything is defined to some extent by the mountains, sea, and unresting skies above.

St Margaret's Well

Turning left by the Palace car park, St Margaret's Well is reached by the low path on the far side of the main park road. Still in a medieval well house, the waters flow but are screened off by a metal grille. The park is full of natural springs and underground streams. Their plentiful supply caused as many problems with the excavation of the Scottish Parliament foundations as the benefits they once supplied to the numerous breweries which existed around Holyrood from the time of the Augustinian monks onwards.

St Margaret was a royal refugee, originally from Hungary and then from the Saxon Court of England. Educated under the saintly and learned influence of Edward the Confessor, Margaret fled northwards by sea after the Battle of Hastings in 1066. With her she brought a precious relic, a fragment of Calvary's Cross embedded in an exquisite ebony crucifix – the holy rood.

Whether by accident or design, Margaret's ship sought refuge from the storms in the Firth of Forth, landing near the then royal capital of Dunfermline. Malcolm King of Scots, who himself had been a refugee at the English Court, came to welcome Margaret and offer her sanctuary. The result was a royal marriage and six children from which most of the subsequent monarchs of Scotland and England came to be descended. Margaret was later canonised because of her untiring work to feed and educate the poor and her assistance to refugees and prisoners of war. In the words of the canonisation address, preserved in the Vatican,

Torn from home, you embrace another
You became Queen and Mother,
The Glory of Scots,
Your crown a Crown of charity,
Your way, the Royal Way of the Cross.

However, there are more levels to the well itself than even Margaret's own rich story which gives Holyrood its name. It was known in medieval times as the Rood Well, but the well house itself was moved here much later from St Triduana's Well. This was an important medieval healing shrine, which can still be visited at St Margaret's Church in nearby Restalrig.

Triduana, sometimes known as Modwenna or Medwana, was an Irish princess who fled to Galloway in Scotland to escape the attentions of an unwelcome suitor. Like many highborn women in the early Christian period, she wanted to live the life of an anchorite or nun, which would probably have been Margaret's own preference had William the Conqueror not intervened. Pressed by her pursuer, whose warrior honour was offended by Modwenna's refusal, she asked him which part of her he most desired. He replied, diplomatically, her eyes. Upon this declaration, Modwenna speared both her eyes on a thorn and handed them over. Unsurprisingly, perhaps, St Triduana's Well became famous for its cures for blindness and eye infections.

Healing takes us deeper into the history of this well for the association between natural sources of water, cleansing and healing is very ancient. The springs and wells of the park are an important part of its relationship with custom and ritual through the centuries, despite the disapproval of the religious and civic authorities.

Not long after the Protestant Reformation of 1560, Ministers and

Kirk Sessions were given the power to punish crimes of sorcery and witchcraft. This may have been a political gesture to appease religious radicals who were disgruntled because the nobility had diverted most of the wealth of the old Church, including the lands of the former Holyrood Abbey, into their own coffers rather than into the good works envisaged by John Knox. But, whatever the reason, this transfer of powers was to have severe consequences.

In the 1570's there was a serving woman, a young widow called Janet Boysman, living in the Canongate. She was a known herbalist so was asked to nurse her neighbour, Allan Anderson, who was poorly with fever. Having tried a number of remedies without success, and with Anderson weakening, Janet resorted to Arthur's Seat by night where at one of its wells, according to her later 'confession', she called on the Holy Ghost, Arthur and his Queen to aid her. Once these words had been uttered, a tall, strongly built man appeared and counselled her to dip Anderson's shirt three times in the waters of the spring and then wrap him in it. This done, the fever was broken and Anderson recovered.

However, this unexpected cure brought Janet's healing activities to the attention of the Kirk. She was arrested, interrogated and executed for the 'crime' of continuing the traditional practice of wise women and healers in her long established culture. The invocation to 'Arthur and his Queen' strikes a genuine note, underlining the importance of the name 'Arthur's Seat' in many of the older stories.

St Margaret's Well continued to be a point of interest for visitors to Edinburgh through the generations. Thomas Guthrie, the mid-Victorian minister and social reformer, recounts bringing guests to the well where some street kids were earning a penny by drawing cups of water for tasting. 'If there was a place,' he asked them, 'where you could go and

be fed and have the chance to learn to read and write, would you go?'.
'Wud I gang?', responded one, 'aye an thoosans wi me!'. Guthrie went
on to found Edinburgh's Ragged Schools, taking many uncared-for
youngsters off the streets.

Heart of Midlothian

Going up by the side of the well onto the upper path, you begin to
move away from the grassy flats onto the first lower slopes. Quickly
you find yourself coming down into a shallow valley where the burn
that feeds St Margaret's Loch runs along the bottom. To your right,
the first ridges are running up into the hidden folds that form the
centre of the park's contours. Ahead, the ground rises steeply to St
Anthony's Well with a small cave behind. To the left, the ground falls
away towards the Loch with St Anthony's ruined chapel standing
sentinel-like above. The well is another of the park's sacred springs
and an ideal spot for the cleansing rituals of Mayday or Beltane,
as described by Robert Fergusson in the 18th century.

> On May Day in a fairy ring,
> We've seen them round St Anton's spring,
> Frae grass the caller dewdrops wring
> To weet their een
> And water clear as crystal spring
> To synd them clean

Though these customs were officially discouraged through the
centuries, they have recently re-emerged in the form of a modern
Beltane Festival on Calton Hill which marks the beginning of summer.
But many still come quietly to the hidden interiors of Arthur's Seat to
renew their Mayday bond with nature's mysteries.

Quickly and suddenly we lose the sense of city. Though the park is now surrounded by Edinburgh, it still retains a sense of wildness. Nowadays people forget this and get caught in severe weather or stuck on rock cliffs they considered only a rough scramble. But in past times Arthur's Seat was regarded as wild nature and therefore dangerous. It stood against the civic order of the town. Untamed creatures might roam here and it was a haunt of outlaws and those who sought refuge from the cruelties of social and political oppression.

This is the backdrop to Sir Water Scott's defining Edinburgh novel, *The Heart of Midlothian*, which is set in the early 18th century not long after the 1707 Union of the Scottish and English Parliaments in London. The story involves political riot, lynch mobs and smugglers who are heroes to some and criminals to others. But at the centre of the story are the two daughters of Davie Deans, the shepherd on Arthur's Seat who lives at St Leonard's Bank on the southwest edge of the park.

The younger daughter, Effie, is 'the Lily of St Leonard's', a beauty who falls for one of the smugglers, Robert Wilson. He has been a leading figure in the riots but manages to escape custody in the town jail, the Tolbooth. Effie has a child by Wilson but the baby disappears soon after birth. Because Effie told no-one she was pregnant, she falls under the cruel 'Law Of Concealment' and is herself imprisoned in the Tolbooth – the 'Heart of Midlothian'. She is tried for her life. Wilson wants Effie's older sister, Jeanie Deans, to testify that her sister had confided in Jeanie about the pregnancy, so allowing her to be acquitted. But Jeanie, like her father, is an earnest Presbyterian who cannot lie on oath.

A desperate Wilson, now on the run, makes a tryst with Jeanie on the wild fringes of the park by night. Drawing a loaded pistol, he threatens to kill her unless she agrees to testify, but Jeanie faces him down. Subsequently she walks all the way to London to plead a royal pardon for her sister who has now been condemned to hang.

The fate of Effie's child remains unknown but it seems likely that the baby had been murdered by one of the criminal fraternity, a notorious old woman called Meg Murdockson. Meg herself had a daughter who lost her baby, perhaps by the same hand, and wanders Arthur's Seat distraught looking for her child. This is the Ophelia-like figure of Madge Wildfire, singing snatches of old ballads.

> I am Queen of the Wake, and I'm Lady of May,
> And I lead the blithe ring round the Maypole today,
> The wild-fire that flashes so fair and so free,
> Was never so bright or so bonny as me.

Or in more typically fey and melancholy vein,

> Proud Maisie is in the wood,
> Walking so early,
> Sweet Robin sits on the bush,
> Singing so rarely.
> Tell me thou bonny bird,
> When shall I marry me?
> When six braw gentlemen
> Kirkward shall carry ye.

Though Jeanie succeeds in winning a pardon, Effie's life is cast under a shadow of sadness and she too is fated to haunt Arthur's Seat.

> Arthur's Seat shall be my bed,
> No sheets will e'er be pressed by me,
> St Anton's Well will be my drink,
> Since my true love's forsaken me.

Despite being fictional, the characters and events of *Heart of Midlothian* have entered the popular lore and legend of the park. Scott captures perfectly the dramatic contrasts of the landscape, as well as the tensions between order and conflict both in nature and human society. Walking up the Royal Mile by St Giles Cathedral, you can see a Heart of Midlothian in the setts, or paving stones, marking the site of the former prison. A true son or daughter of Auld Reekie is supposed to spit on it as they pass by. The past is always beneath our feet, and when the paving stones were being re-laid the Tolbooth's forbidding foundation stones were exposed to view.

The Antlers and The Cross

Having paid your respects at the stone bowl of St Anton's Well, which is marked by a large boulder on the slope ahead (no spitting required here), there is a choice of routes. You can climb through the central valleys of the park, like the journey followed by Stuart McHardy in the latter half of the book, rising eventually after many ups and downs to the summit of Arthur's Seat. Our circuit, however, continues by way of St Margaret's Loch and then sunwise and seaward round the hill. Traditionally it was always considered lucky to go sunwise, *deasail*, as opposed to the other direction, *widdershins*, which was associated with evil magic.

St Margaret's Loch is much favoured by swans and, to a lesser extent, geese. The park is rich in bird life but each species has its favourite haunt. The loch is a manmade creation, covering what was once low-lying boggy ground densely populated by bushes and trees which stretched back towards Holyrood. Here, the deer and wild boar that were bred for the park ran free awaiting pursuit by the royal hunt.

It was Holy Cross Day, 14 September as it falls still in the Roman Catholic calendar, when David I of Scotland was resident in his royal Castle of Edinburgh. Early in the morning, the King attended Mass in the little wooden chapel which had been built for David's pious mother, Queen Margaret. She herself had died in the castle holding her sacred relic, the Holy Rood.

On that 14 September, it was a glorious sunny morning imbued with the clear eastern light which Edinburgh often enjoys, with a wave of September warmth as a bonus. The lords and knights of David's Court were champing at the bit to go hunting in the royal park but the King's religious advisers, who included leading figures in reforming European monasticism, forbade such worldly pursuits on this holy feast day.

'Your Majesty,' they remonstrated, 'what kind of example will it set your people if you go clattering down the High Street intent on pleasure when all should be on their knees before the holy altar?'

David was a pious king, later described by James V as 'a sair sanct for the croun' because of his many gifts to the Church of royal lands and money, but on this occasion he failed to resist natural temptation. At the head of a troupe of richly caparisoned horsemen, he cantered out of the castle and down the High Street of Edinburgh, in full view of his admiring rather than censorious subjects. Then, gathering speed, they thundered through the Netherbow Port, down what is now the Canongate, and into the royal hunting park.

Mounted on his magnificent white stallion, King David showed his mettle as a rider by getting ahead of the rest. Somewhere on the flat, the hunt startled a magnificent twelve pointer stag which turned and ran. Horns sounded, hounds were loosed and horses spurred into headlong chase.

By now David was well out in front, and pursued the magnificent quarry into the shrubs and stunted trees which covered the low lying boggy ground at the foot of the hill. But in a clearing amongst these thickets, the stag turned at bay. David's stallion reared; he was thrown winded to the ground. Before the King could regain his feet, the huge stag put down his antlers and thrust them furiously forward to gore his fallen pursuer. In desperate self-defence David put out his hands in a vain effort to hold off those ferocious tines. But as he grasped the antlers a cross appeared between his hands, glinting in the sunlight. The stag drew back, turned and cantered off through the wood.

Much shaken, King David returned to the castle. That night he dreamed of founding an Abbey at the entrance to the royal hunting park. This monastery would be dedicated to the memory of his mother Margaret and of her precious ebony cross – the Haly Rude or Holy Rood. Eventually the Abbey grew into a palace in which the royal Parliament of Scotland's medieval kingdom often met.

The foundation legend of Holyrood Abbey has a slightly 'off the peg' flavour since the same story features in various European locations with different Saints and Kings. However, the essence of storytelling is relocation to a familiar setting and no locale could be more appropriate than Arthur's Seat and Holyrood. In the spirit of Margaret's own piety, the Abbey was officially dedicated to the Holy Rood, St Mary the Virgin and All Saints. Before the Reformation the religious foundation had already given way to the royal palace. Later the Abbey Church became the Chapel Royal.

To the Hill

Symphony for Holyrood

One

andante

Early light to dusk
blanket haared or lucent lensed
on slopes and troughs and rocks
lonely runners
pounding out their beats
wearing down on time worn tracks
single yet in consort dogged to break free.
A common ground to pattern steep and crag
night and day in every weather
till as bird flights criss-cross in season
the hill is flagged with gaudy balloons
soaring kites and billowing marquees.
Light moment of release to drift
above the rocky flanks and scarcely feel
the indentation, no vestige of a beginning
no prospect of an end in moving mass
unmeasured by the individual footfall,
all work is turned to play.
Of these interludes the hill retains
no mark or memory, blows away to sea.
Persistently the folk resume to run
walk or climb unobtrusive to the summit
small scale paths thread through
the wider element, space between
the earth and sky
being air.

Hill of the Dead

At the far end of St Margaret's Loch our circuit turns right and begins
to climb. The trick here is to keep looking back as well as forward
since gradually the unity of Edinburgh's landscape is being laid out
behind you. There is a common confusion that Arthur's Seat is itself
a dormant volcano, when, in fact, it is only one small part of a much
bigger post volcanic landscape. The original volcano was a massive
feature, dwarfing the whole of the present extent of Edinburgh and
all of the city's principal features. The Castle Rock, Calton Hill,
Salisbury Crags and Arthur's Seat are fragmentary remains of the one
geological phenomenon after a millenium of weather has done its work.

This gives Edinburgh its exceptional cityscape which combines
dramatic diversity within a boldly sculpted unity. Looking back,
you see Calton Hill in relation to the other heights and the long
backbone of the Royal Mile rising to Edinburgh Castle. There may
be a glint of sun on spearheads as King David's hunting party gallops
down the route more often reserved for stately processions. We shall
discover later that the earliest myths surrounding Arthur's Seat concern
the formation of this landscape. In the words of Cuthbert Day's rather
earnest poem 'Arthur's Seat – A Ruined Volcano', it is a worthy thing
to search 'the mystery of a verdant hill, to find that fire...

> Here once burst forth; the rocks were rent
> And molten lava like a fiery flood
> Stream'd o'er the land. That here a mound
> In noble lion form was raised
> As watch and ward, a sentinel
> Over all Midlothian's bounds

We are climbing steadily now in a clockwise direction. On the right

hand, the slopes comprise rough tussocky moorland rising to the Whinny Hill, also known as the Fairy Knowe; on the left, gradually regenerating woods are creeping up the hillside. Several gates and paths breach the park wall giving access for all those who live around the Seat. Walkers and runners abound at all hours of the day. But the park has for centuries been the local place to go on holidays and festivals. And it has often been a resort of children looking for adventure and play, officially or unofficially.

Early in the 19th century two young boys came into the park as normal to roam and dream. Their exact route is unknown but somewhere on Whinny Hill, above us on the north east slopes, they stumbled into a strange discovery. The ground seemed to have given way under a foothold and a shallow cavity was exposed. Rummaging in the hole the boys found 17 little coffins, their lids ornamented with tiny tin panels. Within each one was placed a carefully, if rather crudely, carved doll. They took their discovery back to the adult world and eventually nine of the little coffins found a place in Scotland's National Museum, where they can still be seen today. But when had they been placed there and why?

Naturally, speculation ranged over witchcraft, voodoo curses and so forth. *The Scotsman* ascribed the dolls in January 1836, soon after their discovery, to 'the infernal hags of Arthur's Seat'. However, each of the little figures was respectfully and carefully placed with no pins, nails, deforming marks or other evidence of malign intention. More recent anthropological investigation has provided a persuasive explanation which is superbly popularised by the contemporary Scottish novelist Ian Rankin in his haunting Inspector Rebus novel *The Falls*.

At the start of the 19th century, Edinburgh was one of the world's leading centres of medical science and research. Medical advancement needed human bodies for dissection, but religious belief and popular prejudice were united in opposition to such a fate for any human being other than an executed criminal. Consequently, an illegal trade opened up in excavating recently buried corpses for clandestine sale to the anatomists.

Two itinerant Irish labourers, Burke and Hare, had come to Scotland to work on the Union Canal. Soon they were involved in the much more lucrative grave robbing trade, smuggling excavated corpses from country areas into the city on canal boats. This, however, was a risky and laborious operation, and all over Scotland armed guard was being mounted in kirkyards to scare off the 'resurrectionists'.

Soon the two men, who had taken up lodgings in Edinburgh, hit on a more convenient supply chain. They turned their attention to the city's poor and unregistered; those of no fixed address or abode, those who, as prostitutes, landless tramps, hawkers and Travelling People, belonged nowhere that might especially remember or claim them.

Murder offered a much easier means of securing the freshest possible human bodies with minimum transport costs. It was cunning, ruthless and immoral capitalism. Burke and Hare began to prey on the isolated and vulnerable people of both sexes living in the crowded anonymous slums of the old city. From there, once dispatched, they could easily be delivered by way of underground vaults and passages to the Infirmary, where anatomists, such as the famous Dr Robert Knox, did not enquire too closely into the human identity of the corpses whose innards they were keen to explore.

> Up the close and doon the stair
> But an Ben wi Burke and Hare
> Burke's the butcher, Hare's the thief
> Knox the boy wha buys the beef.

By the time Burke and Hare were caught it is believed that at least 17 vulnerable souls had fallen victim to their rough trade. Seventeen unburied bodies – 17 unrestful spirits. So in restitution someone gave each a symbolic burial on the sacred hill, laying them to rest.
The preservation of the wooden coffins and figures, though some were already rotting, makes complete sense if they had only been buried years rather than centuries previously. It is a convincing explanation, and one that accords with the underlying folk reverence for Arthur's Seat that characterises people's attitude through the millennia. Moreover, the tinwork on the coffin lids is reminiscent of Scottish Gypsy-Travellers who were traditionally tinsmiths. They had an especial horror of 'the Burkers', which continues in their stories to the present day, believing that many of their nomadic kin were counted amongst the victims.

Hare turned Queen's evidence, which is why we know the likely number of their victims, and Burke went to the gallows. There is a local tradition in remote Applecross in the western Highlands that Hare eked out the remainder of a miserable existence there under an assumed name. Perhaps that was a fitting punishment for someone who had callously stripped so many of their personal identity.

Firth and Frontier

Continuing our ascent round the shoulder of Whinny Hill, the sight-lines to our left open dramatically first to the Forth estuary and then out to the North Sea. It comes almost as a shock that, having been encompassed by valley and hill, we are suddenly exposed to sea and sky in this way. But Edinburgh is a city by the sea, and the whole northern flank of Arthur's Seat has salt water in its view. Ahead we can also make out the small peak of Dunsapie Hill and, progressively closer, the two central peaks of Crow Hill and the Seat itself. All three show evidence of fortification.

This a good stance from which to understand Arthur's Seat as a beacon hill and a frontier fortress. For many centuries, the River Forth divided the British tribes of southern Scotland from the related but different peoples of the north who are now known as Picts, though this name may once have referred to all the peoples north of Hadrian's Wall.

Arthur's Seat and Edinburgh Castle were at one time citadels of the Gododdin (*Votadini* in Latin) who occupied territories equivalent to the later Lothians. Allied to the Britons of Strathclyde but fighting and raiding against Scots in the west and Picts to the north, the Gododdin eventually succumbed to the military and trading muscle of the Northumbrian Kingdom to the south. Northumbria was ruled by Anglo-Saxon speakers who had originally arrived as Roman mercenaries to man Hadrian's Wall, and retained strong connections across the North Sea.

These crosscurrents and conflicts influenced Scotland's political and cultural fate from long before the Roman occupation, and reasserted themselves after the early Roman withdrawal. Arthur's Seat was literally in the centre of the action, and bears evidence of defensive structures from different periods facing in every direction. These structures probably had ritual as much as military functions. From where we stand we can see the fort on Dunsapie Hill which faces south and the extensive northlands of the Picts beyond the firth. In the early centuries before and after Christ, this must have been an anxious outlook, requiring all the religious and symbolic support of this sacred site, as well as the beacon fires that could run east to Traprain and Berwick Law or back, according to the source of danger.

One invaluable frontier story survives from this period because of its connection with a Christian saint and later Church traditions. This story happens in a series of locations that are before our eyes. Tennoch (sometimes Thenew or Enoch) was the daughter of Lot, Chief of the Gododdin. In the normal run of custom and alliance, he had decreed that she should marry her cousin Ewan or Owen, son of the Chief of Strathclyde. But Tennoch had fallen under the influence of a community of holy women in East Lothian led by an Irish Abbess. In addition, according to the traditional medieval genealogies, Tennoch was a niece of Arthur through her mother Anna, and had been partly educated at his Christian Court. Consequently she refused, desiring the life of religion in preference to traditional marriage.

Infuriated by her refusal, Lot sent his daughter away from his citadel at Traprain Law, which can be seen to the east, into the Lammermuirs to herd pigs till she would see sense. Tennoch remained obdurate. Then fate intervened in the shape of Ewan, the slighted betrothed. Whether offended or desirous or both, he tracked Tennoch down and tried to win her round without success, finally resorting to violence and rape. In consequence, Tennoch became pregnant and was brought back to Traprain to face the patriarchal music.

First, Lot instructed his people to stone her to death on the hilltop. But in a direct echo of the Gospel story of Jesus and the woman charged with adultery, the people refused, dropping their rocks and stones. Next he had Tennoch bound in a ritual chariot and hurled off the steep cliff face. But miraculously the axle remained unbroken and, though bruised and shaken, Tennoch survived. Finally, having apparently learned nothing from these lessons, Lot had his daughter put in a *curragh*, or *coracle*, without oar or sail and shoved out to sea at Aberlady. This was regarded in early Celtic cultures as a particularly cruel punishment, leading inevitably to a lingering death from thirst and starvation.

But those who handed this story down are with Tennoch, describing how all the fish, dolphins, seals, porpoises and sea birds followed in the wake of her little vessel so that no marine harvest was ever again landed at that place. The tide carried a forlorn Tennoch out towards the open sea but the *curragh* grounded on The Isle of May at the mouth of the Forth estuary. On a clear day, this long cliff-bound island can be seen on the horizon from Arthur's Seat. Possibly meaning Island of Maidens, the May Isle was a religious sanctuary blessed with a fresh-water spring so Tennoch was able to drink and wait for the turn of the tide. Medieval pilgrims still travelled to the May seeking the spring waters as a cure for infertility.

The returning tide then carried the courageous Tennoch back upriver across our present view, round by Edinburgh and Leith, eventually touching land at Culross on the north side of the river. St Margaret was later to be driven by a storm on the same course to the nearby refuge of Dunfermline. By this time darkness was falling and Tennoch was exhausted and frozen. With her remaining strength, she managed to crawl onto the now deserted beach. The monks of Culross had been working on the shore and had smoored a fire there. Tennoch was able to uncover the ashes and stir the fire back to life, saving herself and her baby who was born through the night. The next morning the monks found mother and child on the shore and brought them to their Abbot, St Serf. When he heard her story he granted them refuge.

Tennoch's child grew up to be St Kentigern or Mungo, founder of Glasgow in Strathclyde, while Tennoch finally achieved her wish by becoming a leader of the early church and founder in her own right of a religious community at Loch Lomond. Both Tennoch and Mungo are still commemorated at Glasgow Cathedral. Though this tale is layered with later hagiography, it retains authentic traces of its origins and is clearly written in the landscape before our eyes. Before books and literacy, stories were intertwined in the memory with places; the more special the place, the richer and more numerous the tales.

The Men of The North

It is hard to turn your back on the magnificent view stretching before us from river to firth to sea. But either wind or time moves you on into the gully between Dunsapie Hill and the peaks, leaving the sea behind. There is something slightly eerie about this transition. You know you are high up yet suddenly you are enclosed, often in shadow, and sometimes the wind funnels through this narrow passage with a plaintive howl. If one of the old names for Arthur's Seat is *Craigenmaf*, 'Hill of the Dead', then some of those departed spirits seem to be intently present. There is an unexpected chill even on a warm day.

Within the gully or pass there is an excellent view of the ramparts and terraces surrounding the twin summits. Whether these large scale constructions were ceremonial, military or agricultural is now almost impossible to say. Perhaps they were a mixture of all three. But this severe hanging valley has the sense of a place where people exercised, trained and tested themselves, and still do. Feats of arms and of endurance were prepared on these heights which are not for the casual tourist but the seriously challenged. Prince Albert wanted to establish a tearoom here for those circuiting the hill but thankfully failed.

One military expedition that began from Edinburgh is recorded in the ancient elegiac poem 'The Gododdin'. The work is ascribed to the Welsh poet Aneirin and forms part of the tradition of 'The Men of the North' which belongs to southern Scotland and northern England. These traditions were later preserved in Wales which became the last stronghold of the older British culture. In 'The Gododdin', 363 chosen champions and allies gather to prepare for a battle against the Anglo-Saxons of Northumbria. With perhaps a degree of poetic licence, the preparations continue for a year with martial exercise, confessions and masses, feasting, music and storytelling.

> Men went to Catraeth, they were renowned
> Wine and mead from gold cups was their drink
> A year in noble ceremonial
> Three hundred and sixty three gold-torqued men
> Out of Eidin's bright fortress.
> Men went to Catraeth at dawn
> High spirits lessened their lifespan
> They drank mead, gold and sweet, ensnaring,
> For a year the minstrels were merry
> In Eidin's great hall

So far so good. Who could fail to sign up for this kind of campaigning? But before all the festivities in the great hall on the Castle Rock, there was some hard training to be done, probably on and around Arthur's Seat. And later, according to Aneirin, some seriously bloody fighting followed. We owe this fine version of a very difficult early text to poet and scholar Jospeh P. Clancy.

> Men went to Catraeth with a war cry,
> Speedy steeds and dark armour and shields,
> Spear-shafts held high and spear-points sharp-edged,
> And glittering coats-of-mail and swords.
> Ringed round a rampart of shields

Sharp they press the attack, seize plunder,
Loud as thunder the crashing of shields
Ripped and pierced with spear-points.
Deep in blood blades butchered
In the strife, heads under hard iron,
Great hosts would groan.

The poem consists of intensely crafted vignettes of each warrior,
all of whom have been slain. Aneirin remembers the beautiful but
deadly Owen, whose graceful gestures delight and grieve, dealing pallid
death. Then there is the much lamented Geraint whose hospitality and
generosity to the poet was legendary. And there is Gwarrdur, 'who
though he was not Arthur, made his strength a refuge, the front line's
bulwark'. This is the first recorded mention in any known literature
of Arthur, already viewed as a legendary hero, and it is directly
connected with Edinburgh, giving the lie to any suggestion that the
name 'Arthur's Seat' is a later romantic invention. If 'The Gododdin'
originates about 500 CE, it brings us very close to the first cultural
context of the Arthur legends.

'The Gododdin' has a sting in the tail since Aneirin, one of the few
survivors, is imprisoned but then dramatically rescued, as befits
a poet on whose skill the fame of all involved rests. The bardic
voice is sustained even as the Men of the North slip into the mists
of time.

I, not-I, Aneirin
Taliesin knows it
Master of word-craft
Sang to Gododdin
Before the day dawned.

It has generally been assumed that Catraeth refers to Catterick, and that 'The Gododdin' describes an expedition south against the Northumbrians. But it has also been suggested that this battle was closer to home. Perhaps some of the fallen heroes were buried here on Arthur's Seat, the Hill of the Dead. And the sorrowing wind blows on through the gully where the horses raced and spears flashed in the sunlight. But the voice of the bard can still be heard.

Sword in the Loch

Emerging at the other end of the Dunsapie pass, another panorama extends before our eyes. The rolling uplands of southern Edinburgh trace the city's growth, swallowing up historic estates and castles such as Craigmillar's classic motte and bailey which played an important part in the life of Mary Queen of Scots. It was here that the plot to murder her estranged husband Darnley was supposedly hatched. To the west, the Pentlands provide a boundary between Mid and West Lothian but the focus of our attention is much closer at hand. Directly below is Duddingston Village which is connected through the kirklands of Duddingston to the Loch, a lucent oval tucked below the Hill.

Duddingston Loch is the principal natural water source in the park. It is fed by burns from several directions and fringed with woods, marshes and meadows. Ducks and geese populate the loch while on the far side the herons have carved out their own distinctive territory. The name Duddingston is supposedly Norman – the settlement of Doddin – but masks an older identity. A Chronicle kept by the Cistercian monks of Melrose preserves the name as Tref-yr-Linn –

the settlement by the lake. This transports us back into the old British world of 'The Gododdin'.

Looking down from on high we can trace a very ancient pattern. While Arthur's Seat was the locale of military and aristocratic power, the religious settlement of Tref-yr-Linn was nearby. It is close enough to provide appropriate religious backing but not so close as to constrain a degree of religious, sexual and moral flexibility. The religious caste – druids and then priests – was an essential channel of power and prestige, but the clergy were uncomfortable bedfellows when it came to the messy flow of everyday life. This conjunction of the military seat of power with an adjacent religious community recurs in many parts of Scotland.

There are other riches here as well. The medieval parish church is flanked by an erstwhile field and by the minister's glebe or pasture, both sloping down to the loch. It is all visible here beneath us like a Google map in three dimensions. In the late 20th century, two Doctor Neills, husband and wife, began transforming the Calves Field below the Kirk into a superb landscape garden, bordering the extensive manse garden. Now there are also plans to add the glebe to this renascent 21st century greenscape. On the boundary line between glebe and garden stands the Thomson Tower, in which the 19th century painter and minister John Thomson created outstanding landscape art. It is now a Museum of Curling, since the rules of this very Scottish (and now international) sport were first formalised here where the loch provided an outstanding field of play.

On the other side of the Kirk lies the village of Duddingston – the actual Tref-yr-Linn. It has its own rural character even within the city. Bonnie Prince Charlie stayed here, his army bivouacking on Arthur's Seat, the night before his famous victory at Prestonpans in East

Lothian. The Sheep Heid Inn in Duddingston is the oldest pub in Edinburgh, and a very convenient resting point on this journey.

Depending on your motivation, it is decision time on routes. You could either take a shortcut back to Edinburgh on this upper road, the Queen's Drive. By this route you get a superb view of what Robert Louis Stevenson called 'my precipitous city', climbing by roofs and gables up to the castle. Alternatively, descend steeply by the hill path on the left and then the steps of Jacob's Ladder to Duddingston itself. Our circuit is by way of Duddingston. Tread carefully on both the path and the steps of the Ladder, especially in damp weather.

The effort of descent is well rewarded as you reach the sheltered haven of Tref-yr-Linn. Make first for the lochside where you experience yet another of the scenic transformations typical of the park. There is an intimacy and seductive gentleness about this ancient lake which attracts all ages onto its margins to feed the birds or simply watch wind and light play on the surface. The loch has moods for all seasons – the cold and ruffled, the sparkling and sunny, the frozen fastness of deep winter. But the transforming magic comes by moonlight, when a luminous goddess repossesses the deeps and we realise we are all still participants in the mystery of nature.

In the 18th century, a large hoard of Bronze Age swords and spears was dredged from the loch. There was also evidence of some kind of wooden platform or jetty. Some phlegmatic archaeologists have suggested that these discoveries might represent disposal of waste from a smithy on the hill above the loch. Scrap of this scale would clearly have been recycled in the forge, not dumped, while the reverence for natural water sources was deeply engrained in Celtic culture. Instead, these could be interpreted as precious offerings made to the goddesses of the lake. We are looking at an important site of primal religion –

a sacred linn, or pool, amidst the many sacred springs. The continuity is visible here right through to the medieval and modern parish church – the chapel by the lake.

Stillness is often a feature of the loch in its sheltered neuk. The trees that ring its shores are reflected on the surface surrounding the sky above and below. At dawn, or even more at twilight, the abundant bird life of this wildlife sanctuary evokes the mood: the silent rhythm of a long winged hunting heron; the whirr of the ducks; the erratic high speed flight of bats; the heavy landing of a greylag or barnacle goose; the majestic beat of swan's wings over the waters. Soon, a white moon slips out between the clouds to shine its path over the lake.

There is an obvious story suggested by this locale, one much evoked and ornamented by Tennyson.

> So all day long the noise of battle roll'd
> Among the mountains by the winter sea
> Until King Arthur's Table, man by man
> Had fallen in Lyonesse about their Lord.

When at last the traitor Mordred falls, slain by his own king and uncle in mortal combat, Bedivere, last of the knights, takes up his wounded Lord and carries him to a chapel by a lakeside near the field of battle. The mortally wounded Arthur tells Bedivere to take his sword Excalibur.

'I received it from the water and to the water it should be returned. Watch what you see and bring me word'.

So Bedivere takes Excalibur and stepping from the ruined shrine he follows the winding path to 'the shining levels of the lake'.

Here he stops. Drawing the sword from its scabbard, he holds it up to the light by its hilt which is sparkling in the cold moonlight. 'No,' he says, 'this cannot be. My master is not himself', and sheathing the blade he hides it in the rushes and climbs back to the chapel.

'What did you see?' says Arthur.

'I saw nothing but waves and wind.'

'You lie, false knight. Return and do your duty.'

So Bedivere returns, takes hold again of Excalibur and once more draws the blade. 'If this sword is lost,' he muses, fully aware that Arthur is dying, 'how will anyone remember my Lord? What sign or symbol will be left of all that has been achieved and suffered?' So once again he conceals the sword and returns to Arthur.

'What did you see?'

'I heard the ripple washing in the reeds, and the wild water lapping on the rocks.'

'You lie, false knight. Now go back and do my bidding or I will kill you with these bare hands.'

And Arthur rears like a lion, even in his weakened state, wounded yet doubly dangerous.

Back Bedivere goes, swiftly this time, and without thought or hesitation he takes the sword and throws it wheeling high into the night sky. The blade flashes in the moonlight but even before it can strike the water an arm clothed in white rises from the lake, grasps the hilt and waving Excalibur three times sunwise draws it under the water. Bedivere stands in wonder as the ripples fade and the surface become still again.

Then, still in a daze, he goes back for the third time to Arthur and relates what he has seen.

'Good. Now the time has come. Take me to the lochside.'

So Bedivere takes Arthur on his back and, weighed down by his burden, steps gingerly down the crag. The night is closing in hard and cold and his iron-shod heels ring on the rocks.

> And on a sudden lo the level lake
> Then saw they how there hove a dusky barge
> Dark as a funeral scarf from stem to stern
> And all the decks were dense with stately forms
> Black stoled black, hooded like a dream.
> Three queens with crowns of gold
> By these and from them rose
> A cry that shivered to the tingling stars
> And as it were one voice an agony
> Of lamentation like a wind that shrills
> All night in a wasteland, where no-one comes
> Or hath come since the making of the world.

Bedivere lifts Arthur into the barge. Willing hands lower him gently down, loosen his straps and armour and seek out his hurts. The King lies beneath the masts like a shattered column. As the boat puts out again, a breeze fills the sails and a keening rises on the water like a dying swan's last song. Yet is it a death hymn or only a lament at parting, as Arthur is borne to the healing isle of Avalon from where one day he may return?

The faithful Bedivere, last of the fellowship of the Round Table, stands for a long time watching while the hull disappears into the darkness.

The black sails are swallowed up into the horizon and the wailing dies away. Then, climbing slowly, the knight returns to the chapel above the lake. There he finds a hermit bent in prayer over a newly carved tomb.

'Who are you praying for?' asks Bedivere.

'Three women came bearing a corpse. Here they laid him commanding me to pray for his soul.'

'That was my Lord Arthur. Now I must follow your holy calling and stay here to pray. More things are wrought by prayer than this world dreams of'.

Then taking a candle, Bedivere raises it above the tomb lighting up a freshly cut inscription.

> *Hic Iacet Arthurus*
> *Rex Quondam Rexque Futurus.*
> Here lies Arthur
> The Once and Future King.

The Wells O Wearie

A diagonal path leads back up from the lochside through trees and bushes to the main road, so continuing our clockwise journey. The road then narrows into what is called the Windy Gowl and on the left a Hangman's Rock broods over the loch behind us. One unfortunate city hangman is reputed to have hurled himself to his death into the water below here.

Passing through this gully you look down onto the Wells o Wearie, a favoured spot for women coming from the town to wash clothes and socialise while the washing was spread out on the slopes to dry. Over the wall are the grounds of the important historic mansion Prestonfield House. This was built in 1687 as the home of Edinburgh's Lord Provost but was later converted into a hotel. The golf course that now occupies most of the estate shows clear signs of the long rigs which divided up farmland in Scotland until the 18th century improvers swept them away.

In these 'improving' times, it was felt to be beneath the dignity of the royal park to display washing, however clean. Well-doing Victorians cultivated the park as a place for their own wholesome leisure, which required clearing out the messy customs of the poor. Thus began a tidying up exercise over many decades, building paths and fences and discouraging the role of Arthur's Seat as a focus of folk life and tradition. But the park was too big to be strictly controlled, and the songs and stories went on regardless.

> Come let us climb auld Arthur Seat,
> When summer flow'rs are blooming;
> When golden broom and heather bells
> Are a' the air perfuming.
> When sweet May gowans deck the braes,
> The hours flee past fu' cheerie,
> Where bonnie lassies bleach their claes
> Beside the Wells o Wearie!
>
> *The bonnie Wells o Wearie*
> *The bonnie Wells o Wearie*
> *Come let us spend a summer day*
> *Beside the Wells o Wearie!*

The Lily o St Leonard's there
Oft spent a sweet May morning,
Wi' gowans gay and sweet bluebells
Her golden locks adorning.
And there the Laird o Dumbiedykes
Aft gaed to woo his dearie,
And watch his fleecy flocks wi' care,
Beside the Wells o Wearie!

Chorus

There Scotland's Queen in stormy times
Forgot her saddest story;
There brave Prince Charlie led his clans
To deeds of martial glory.
When Johnnie Cope, wi' a' his men
Were scattered tamplinteerie,
There Scotland's banner proudly waved
Beside the Wells o Wearie!

Chorus

Then let us hail auld Arthur Seat:
Like Scotland's rampant lion,
It tow'rs, a wonder of the world,
The wildest storms defyin'.
Wi' dauntless front 'neath summer skies,
Or wintry blasts sae dreary,
It stands in peace or war to guard
The bonnie Wells o Wearie!

Chorus

O lang may bonnie lassies fair
Wi' Nature's charms around them,
Still bleach their claes on flow'ry braes,
Wi' nae sad cares to wound them.
Lang may her sons mid fairy scenes,
Wi' hearts richt leal and cheerie,
Still meet to sing their patriot sangs
Beside the Wells o Wearie!

The bonnie Wells o Wearie
The bonnie Wells o Wearie
Come let us spend a summer day
Beside the Wells o Wearie!

The Sleeping King

On our right hand, close packed basaltic columns tower above the road. Rocks have often been eroded here and crashed down to the Wells. In recent times, work was undertaken to stabilise the cliff face but when this route was no more than a track it could be a dangerous passage, especially by night. That, however, did not prevent bold characters such as Canonbie Dick, the Borders horse trader, from using Arthur's Seat as a shortcut.

Dick had come up to the Musselburgh horse fair and was lodging in Edinburgh. One night he had stayed late in Musselburgh, dealing and drinking, so he took a short cut back round the side of Arthur's Seat. He was leading a magnificent white stallion which he had bought that day at the fair. Suddenly a dark figure appeared on the track in front of him, cloaked and with a hat pulled low over his eyes.

'Dick, Canonbie Dick,' the figure spoke.

'Aye, that's me.'

'What will you take for your horse, Dick?'

'Oh it's not for sale, magnificent beast, light of my eye…'

'Will this be sufficient?'

The man held out a small leather bag – Dick heard the clink and saw the glint of gold – a hundred golden guineas.

'Yes, indeed, well… I might…'

Before Dick could comment or delay the black hooded figure took the bridle, turned and headed round the corner of the hill.

'Wait, stranger, strike the bargain …'

But, as Dick turned the corner, the man had disappeared in the dark leaving the dealer with his bag of gold but no horse. So Dick trudged home.

The next day, he was back at the fair with his surplus funds and purchased another fine stallion. This time he deliberately went home round the hill holding his horse hopefully by the bridle. Sure enough, the cloaked figure appeared on the path once again to bid for the horse with the clink and chink of gold. Dick complied, but this time he insisted on knowing who the stranger was and suggested on going to an inn to seal the bargain. However, this was to no avail as the man turned rapidly into the night and disappeared once again, leaving Dick puzzled but 100 guineas the richer.

So on the third day the bold trader was quick to secure a third fine stallion and, as soon as dusk came in from the sea, he was on the road to Edinburgh. Again the cloaked figure, with the black hat pulled down low on his brow, hailed Dick and bid for the horse – 100 golden guineas.

Dick readily agreed but this time he was determined to go after the man as purchaser with the clinking chinking bags of gold.

'If you won't go with me to the tavern, stranger, let me go with you.'

The figure turned back and stared at Dick from beneath his hat's brim.

'Are you sure that you want to come, Dick?'

'Aye, surely.'

'Then follow.'

The man turned and Dick followed him round the shoulder of the hill. Suddenly they were before an old doorway set in the hillside, all studded with metal nails. It swung open and Dick followed him, puzzled, since he had not seen that door before. Inside, the door opened into a long cavern reaching into the mountain.

All down one side was a row of stalls, each with a white stallion standing quietly. One last stall was empty till the cloaked figure led his final purchase in to complete the row. On the other side, one after another, was a series of stone slabs. On each there lay a knight in full armour, as still as the grave. At the far end of the cavern was a great stone table like an altar.

As Dick looked in amazement the hooded man went to the high table and swept off his hat to reveal flowing white locks and a long white beard.

'Aye, you know me now, Dick. You have come of your own free will and you must make your own choice.'

He pointed to the table where there lay a sword in its scabbard and beside it an old hunting horn.

'Now' said the cloaked figure, 'will you draw the sword or blow the horn?'

Dick hesitated in fear and astonishment. He could blow the horn or perhaps he should draw the sword. But what might happen – would he offend the sleeping warriors? He was not a man of violence but of cunning. Which to choose?

'Choose!' cried Merlin, 'Choose!'

Dick lunged for the horn and blew. A wail of sound filled the cave, echoed and resounded. Candles guttered in a blast of wind. Horses reared and neighed and there was a clash of arms on stone. As Dick felt himself caught up in the wind a great shout roared through the blast.

'Cursed be the man that ever he was born
Who drew not the sword before he blew the horn.'

With a great cry Dick was lifted in the howling gale and swept out of the cave, casting him senselessly on the hillside. The next morning he was found, exposed and feverish. Two shepherds carried him to the Sheep Heid Inn at Duddingston where later that day he died, having related this strange and disturbing tale.

The Giant Edin

Passing on, resist the temptation to explore any recesses in the rock face. We re-emerge into a more open scene with the summits on our right separated by the Gutted Haddie, a ravine cut in the hillside by a landslide. It looks like a fish that has been split open and had its innards scoured out. On our left Pollock Halls, the Edinburgh University residences, occupy the grounds of what was once extended private gardens.

Our circuit goes past the roundabout near the park gates and onto the grass opposite. Ahead is a low grassy ridge that still requires care when taking one of the little paths up. This is the tail end of St Leonard's Bank. Once on the top there is a firm rocky path leading all the way along to the attractive cul-de-sac of St Leonard's Bank, where Jeanie and Effie Deans resided in *Heart of Midlothian*.

About 100 yards along the ridge, stop and look over towards the peaks. This is an excellent viewpoint. On the left hand, the city is spread out with Calton Hill above and the firth expanding out below. On the right you are looking south towards Duddingston Loch with the suburbs of Edinburgh and the Moorfoot Hills beyond. But the immediate drama of this viewpoint is the dominant presence of the Hill itself.

Some have compared Arthur's Seat to a recumbent lion, some to a sleeping giant with a bulbous nose and long beard trailing down Salisbury Crags. But the traditional name of Seat accurately describes the Hill as an elemental vantage point for a god or giant. In his mythic origins, the Arthur hero may have been both god and giant connecting land and sky. Behold his seat, of which there are a number in Scotland, including Ben Arthur in Argyll and Benarty in Fife. They all have a rocky throne on their summits.

The lore of giants concerns elemental forces shaping the landscape.
The Cailleach, or Auld Mither, gives birth to a giant brood who
are fond of chucking rocks to the delight of geologists. She herself
produces rivers and lochs, but is also embroiled in seasonal struggles
between ice and fire as Bride the goddess of spring tries to escape
her wintry clutches. The geologists tell a not dissimilar story about
volcanoes and glaciers.

In the beginning – and before the beginning – misty clouds clung over
the watery land of Lothian, long before it had that name. Lochs and
low marshes held vaporous moisture and all was flat.

This was long, long ago, down aeons and ages of time. The Dun
of Edin, the land of Lothian, was all yet unformed; the coming
of men a millennium away. But in the fiery womb of the world stirred
a mighty giant, waiting to burst into terrible life. The surface of Mother
Earth trembled and shook; ferocious convulsions and contractions sent
shudders over the land. The waters grew to boiling heat and broke in
hissing steam, streaming into the air.

Out of this dense fog, born in plumes of flame, the giant Edin
erupted into life. Cracking open the skin of mother Earth, limb
and body tore itself into the mist-laden light of the sun. And there,
swaddled in blankets of cloud, the giant Edin breathed his fiery
infant breath.

From afar and riding on the cosmic winds, hair streaming in the
howling gale, the jealous Cailleach gazed on the new arrival. This was
the Goddess of Winter, the hag of the ridges who herself had formed
Scotland, dropping great peats from her creel in her lofty dizzy flight.
This was her land and not for the taking.

She scowled upon this upstart giant and sent her freezing gaze into the waters below. Howling in cold rage, her hardening gaze made mountains of ice from the rain and snow.

Yet there was something about this giant form; something that stirred and troubled her. She wanted to subdue but also consume him in her embrace. She waited and watched until, on a sudden impulse, she swooped upon him and folded his fires within her own gaunt, icy frame. For a brief time something blazed and shivered. Then the Cailleach was once more a mountain of ice that clawed and scratched and tore the prostrate giant. Terrible wounds were gouged into his sides and top. Finally she let him sink, silent and defeated, to where he lies in a long and apparently untroubled sleep.

And now you see him still, his giant form spread out. You see him as you journey by the coast road from the south, the sleeping giant, brow to the sky, long body and flanks leaning down towards the sea, his feet sticking from the waters of the Forth and the Island of Inchkeith. He is calm and at peace, it seems. Perhaps he knows that in due course another giant will be born and the passionate struggle will resume. Aeons of time may pass before his rest is disturbed.

But, as you have heard, the echoes and presence of that heroic conflict between the Hag of Ridges and the fiery Edin mysteriously carry their power yet. They pervade the tales of the Dun of Edin, with Arthur's Seat in its heart, making Edinburgh the city of a thousand stories; of fiery deeds and watery tears, of flame and ice, of passions and dreams.

The Gates of Holyrood

Our route continues along the ridge and proceeds along St Leonard's
Bank. Turning left at the end, you will find 'Jeannie Dean's Tryst'
a matter of yards away on the right. The immediate right turn
takes you back into the park down a flight of solid steps through the
wooded slope of the bank.

At the foot, turn left into the shadowy glen below Salisbury Crags.
This is the last leg but the contrasting scenic dramas continue to
impress. On our left the steep flank of St Leonard's Bank is clothed in
burgeoning woods. Ever since the sheep were removed from the park
there has been woodland regeneration round the margins. Davie Deans,
we remember, was the Arthur's Seat shepherd and there were still sheep
pasturing here in the 1970s.

On our right side the barren scree flows down beneath Salisbury Crags,
as if we were halfway up a remote northern mountainside. From this
angle you can barely see the Radical Road which provides safe passage
between scree and crag. There is something glowering and ominous
about this precipitous and treacherous wall of stone. It is a place of
suicide and accidental falls. One lost student was tragically found years
later as a weathered skeleton amidst these stones. On the cliffs above,
James Hogg sets one of the weirdest scenes of his chilling masterpiece,
Private Memoirs and Confessions of a Justified Sinner, where in
a bizarre optical effect the ambiguous hero appears to confront his
double as a gigantic shadow.

It is a relief to emerge once more at the grassy plains of Holyrood with
the hill behind us, our way opening towards sea and sky. Coming out
of the glen we see to our left the local housing area of Dumbiedykes.
At one time, the natural access taken by ordinary people from the town

to the park would be here, avoiding both the palace and the aristocratic mansions in the Canongate. On Mayday, the young came back here bearing their green boughs after bathing in the dew, dancing and ready to perform the Robin Hood plays with merriment and feasting.

Returning to Holyrood, go through the park gates to the foot of the Royal Mile by way of Horse Wynd, between palace and parliament. Turn right into the Abbey Strand which leads to the main gates, now rarely used. You have crossed the sanctuary bounds and cannot be pursued for debt or crime. This tradition outlasted the Abbey, and after the transfer of royal power to London some of the palace buildings were used as a debtors' refuge. The temptation, however, was to go out of an evening drinking in the Canongate. If spotted by bailiffs, pleasure seeking debtors had to run for their freedom which was secure as long as they could get across a stream that ran at the foot of the Strand.

The buildings here retain something of the older character of Holyrood, with its cluster of outbuildings and residences around monastery and palace. Looking through the gates there is a fine view of the ruined Abbey and of the King's Tower, which is the oldest part of the royal apartments. Look left to the guard post, popularly called Queen Mary's Bathhouse, which marks the line of the older palace wall. Here Darnley, Mary's feckless second husband, led the conspirators over to the Tower and up to the Queen's rooms where they butchered the hapless Rizzio. Peaceful now perhaps, but this was once the scene of politics, violence and even murder. Ghosts still walk these parts.

To the right of the gates a striking stone panel adorns the Abbey Strand displaying the royal arms of Mary's father, James v. This magnificently gilded lion and unicorn suggests a last story, often told by Duncan Williamson, one of the great tradition bearers of Scotland's Travelling People. I am not sure if Duncan ever told his story on this spot, though he did have another favourite tale about the Tinker (the Gypsy-Traveller) at the palace gates who outwits and instructs the King. It is all a matter of the right place for the right story, or the right story for the right place.

Long ago, when Scotland was a network of extended family groups living from the rich fruits of land and sea, there was a chief who loved hunting. Such chiefs are called kings in the stories, but really they were first among equals, father to their kin, and often guided by the wise mothers of the tribe.

Now this particular King was a generous breadwinner. He hunted for the love of the chase, but most of all to feed his people. Deer, boar, hare, and the ancient aurochs were all harvested. The people lived well, working hard but feasting, storytelling and singing through the changing seasons.

One day the King went hunting once more in the forests around his village. As the woods became denser, he dismounted from his horse and moved ahead of his men into the dark heart of the wood. Suddenly, in a secluded clearing, he came upon a great bear. The bear reared up in fury, ready to attack. Without hesitation the king notched an arrow on the string, drew his bow and loosed the arrow, all within seconds. The shaft sang true, sinking its point straight into the great bear's chest.

But the bear did not fall. As he raised a huge paw to cover his hurt, he gazed straight into the hunter's eyes. It was as if his gaze went right into the human's soul. They stood locked intensely in this look; it seemed as if there was eternal sadness in the soft brown eyes. Then they misted over and the bear toppled to the ground dead. The hunters rushed into the clearing, whooping in triumph. But the bow fell from the King's hands and without a word he turned on his heel, mounted his waiting horse and rode back to the village.

Arriving at his homestead, the King walked through to the back chamber and slumped in a seat beside the fire. He stared into the flames without acknowledging or speaking to anyone. When the rest of the hunting party arrived back he took no interest in the skinning of the great bear, or in the cooking, carving and eating of its magnificent frame. Even when they spread the hide of the great bear on the floor of the feasting hall their Chief displayed not even a flicker of attention.

Soon people began to worry. The King seemed deep in depression. He refused to go hunting; he barely bothered to eat. He took no part in social and family life. Even his beloved wife was neglected and ignored. She gave the King lots of cuddles and gentle kisses, brought in tasty foods, storytellers and huntsmen ready to leave on the chase. It was no use. Her husband remained sunken in gloom and torpor.

This was getting serious. It was affecting the wellbeing and happiness of a whole people. How could they live if there was no hunting, fishing and adventure? So all the wise men were consulted and when they mumbled and snuffled in their grey beards without result, the Queen turned to the wise women, the ancient ones of the forest. They were so old and full of wisdom that they remembered even the days of the giants.

'Well dear,' they counselled, 'his body's whole but there's something wounded in his spirit because he killed the great bear. So we'll need to come up with some healing... something special.'

'A marvellous creature from the forest,' said one.

'Yes,' said another, 'with the strength of a lion.'

'And the courage and fierceness of the wild boar,' said the third.

'What about speed?' asked the Queen, 'to challenge the hunters?'

'Yes, of course,' chuckled the third old crone, 'we'll give it the swiftness of the fastest horse. Don't you worry, lass, we'll soon have your man working again.'

And off they went, cackling and cracking jokes fit to make a queen blush.

So between them, somewhere in the depths of the mountain where the cauldron of life still bubbles and brews, they made a fabulous creature. This wonder had the haunches and tail of the lion for strength, the lean supple legs and body of the fastest horse, and the tusk of the wild boar planted on its brow for fierceness and courage. As they let their creation loose to run in the forest they said that people would come to call it 'unicorn', after its single horn.

It was not long before rumours of this creature reached the village. An extraordinary marvel, people said, with a golden tail, white body, and a single silver horn. Soon there were definite sightings. The hunts-men came to tell the King. The first time he barely seemed to listen. The second time a flicker of interest stirred in his eyes. But when, on the third visit, the hunters swore they could not keep pace with the creature's speed, he leapt to his feet, called for his fastest horse and charged off into the forest with the surprised but delighted huntsmen trailing behind.

By the second day, they had caught a distant glimpse, and on the third, after a definite sighting, they gave vigorous chase. And so it went on day after day. The creature was simply too fast. It began to seem as if the beast was deliberately showing itself to them, inciting pursuit to flaunt its speed, strength and courage, but always defying their best efforts. Nonetheless the King was now fully restored to health, fired up with the excitement of the chase, and once more providing game in abundance to feed and feast his people. Yet at the feasts every story came back round to the fabulous, yet wholly elusive, creature of the forest and a dreamy look would come into the King's sparkling eyes.

Then one morning the King did not go out hunting as usual. Instead he summoned his counsellors and cunning craftsmen.

'You all know,' he said, 'about the magical creature of the forest. It has the strength of the lion, the courage of the wild boar, and such speed in its long legs and lithe body that it cannot be caught.'

They all murmured their assent and their respectful sympathy that the creature had not yet been caught. Yet at the same time they all expressed their firm belief that such a great hunter as their Chief would soon slay the creature.

'No,' said the King. 'I have realised there are some things that are not made to be captured or slain. The unicorn must remain free and unattainable. But in order that such a marvel may never be forgotten, I would like you to carve the creature and to limn the curves of your carving with rich colours. Instead of subduing this marvellous animal we will echo it through the wonder of your art. Then I will place the creature at the gate of my homestead so that even when I am old and unable to hunt, the unicorn will still be alive for me and for everyone who comes after me.'

The craftsmen were delighted with the King's idea so they fashioned a marvellous unicorn and painted its curving forms in rich colours, gilded with gold and silver. The King placed their skilled work at the gates of his homestead where you can see it right here today. As for the fabulous creature, it is running free still in our spirits and imagination.

So we thank all of the poets, artists, and storytellers such as Duncan Williamson, who have remembered the coming of the unicorn and opened these gates of wonder for following generations.

As for us, our circle now is complete; for today at least. It is time to return home to house, hotel, lodgings, castle or palace. However this is a journey you can repeat endlessly and never exhaust its treasury of delights and surprises. The Hill is never the same twice over. We will always encounter fresh perspectives and epiphanies in this landscape, ever old and ever new.

To the Hill
Symphony for Holyrood
Two
adagio

On the hill in every weather
no two hours alike air in motion,
cloud form dampening smoothing
steady soak of rain, bake of sun,
the scar of wind and hail,
or mantling of the pure white snow.
The hill is veined by hidden routes,
springs and streams between beds of rock,
seeps out the boggy gathering
to dam, drain to lochs.
Beneath each shifting water
tone of vegetation, the latent build
in sweeping crags, bony ribs and outcrops
around the cumulated hump of strength
deceptively worn down, resurgent
in new light to mount and crest.
On the lowest gentle slopes a sandstone
palace nestles with coned towers and gardens.
From St Margaret's Well the intricate
stone weaving traces rise
above the ancient seat of royal parliament and power,
stone to memorialise a sacred cross
and for a time endure.

Along the track another sandstone growth
St Anthony's light looks out to sea
a beacon crumbling above the loch
on which swans glide and wheel in ordered grace
to lift wing westward, Tir nan Og
where faithful spirits are forever free.
The shoulder of the hill turns always seawards,
climb sunwise round the flanks to think and walk,
till Dunsapie and the lion's peak appear
ringed with terraces, the spiral markings
ramparts rubbed away, and undersides
of homesteads like upturned boats
cooried down beneath the storm.
Human habitation eroding centuries restore
to the hill without demur or degradation.
Wind ripples through the pass of shadows
a shiver on the upper loch
between the summits guardians
watch you like herons in the reeds,
stony spirits till they flap disturbed
languorously away, intent on quiet fishing.

Part II:

Evocations of Arthur's Seat

Journey to the Centre

Edinburgh is a city built on hills – Castle Rock, Calton Hill, Blackford Hill, the Braid Hills and Arthur's Seat. Few cities have such a variety of undeveloped spaces and Arthur's Seat in particular provides a sense of wildness right in the heart of the city. In olden times, this was a place for wild revelry, private ritual and a retreat from the Old Town itself. Standing in the Hunter's Bog with the Salisbury Crags to the west, Dasses to the east and the great summit crag rising above, you could be deep in the Highlands. There is no sight and very little sound of the modern cityscape all around.

Throughout Scotland, it used to be the practice that areas of land would be set aside and not cultivated. Such places were generally called the Guidman's, or Halyman's, Croft. The Guidman here is the Devil, who in Scottish tradition is more like Pan, the God of animals, than Satan the personification of evil in Christian tradition. By leaving aside such bits of land dedicated to Auld Cloutie, or Auld Hornie as he was known, it was believed, or certainly hoped, that he would be satisfied and not turn his attention to the precious crops and animals around. It is perhaps not stretching too far a point to see Arthur's Seat as Edinburgh's Guidman's Croft. And this link to practices from the past is telling, for the history of Arthur's Seat itself is suggestive of centuries, and perhaps even millennia, of cultural continuity.

The name of Arthur's Seat takes us back to the dawn of the seventh century in Edinburgh. While the name might not show up in written literature till centuries later, the name of Arthur is entrenched in our oldest literary tradition. The poem 'The Gododdin', written in the closing years of the sixth century, describes a battle undertaken by a group of heroic warriors who, before setting out on their tragic expedition, spent up to a year feasting, telling stories and carousing on the Castle Rock. As mentioned in the first part of this book the warriors of the Gododdin were the tribal people living here when the Romans came north on their first vain attempt to conquer this land. The Roman invaders, who spent so much blood, sweat and tears trying vainly to conquer the native tribes, called them the Votadini. Like the Britons to the west in Strathclyde and their Pictish cousins to the north, they were a warrior people who spoke a form of language called P-Celtic that survives in the modern world as Welsh and Breton. In the great epic poem that tells of the almost total annihilation of the Gododdin warrior band, who fought on and on against overwhelming numbers till only their bard was left to tell the tale, we hear of Gwarrdur. He was a great warrior who, 'though he fed the ravens, was no Arthur'. The motif of feeding the ravens is one that resounds throughout epic poetry of the Celto-Germanic world, and the reference to Arthur tells us little but suggests much. Gwarrdur is a great warrior but still not comparable to Arthur, a warrior of almost god-like status.

Clearly, the poet Aneurin needs to say no more than his name for his audience to know what was meant, and nearly a millennium and a half later the idea of this mysterious but powerful figure still grips the imagination. All tales, legendary, mythic or simply entertaining, belong to the landscape in which they are told. This is how oral tradition works. It makes no sense to relocate the stories of your culture to a different setting, particularly if they are being used to educate children as these often were. So here, as in all the other locations where the Arthurian tales continued to be told, they are truly authentic. The people here believed in Arthur. And in the story of the sleeping warriors inside the very heart of the hill, that several of my friends heard as a child from their parents or grandparents, we see a potential link with the very far past.

The language that the Gododdin spoke was a P-Celtic one, the language of the Gaels of Scotland being like Irish and Manx, known as Q-Celtic. Today the P-Celtic languages are Welsh, Breton and Cornish, and the Welsh see 'The Gododdin' as the oldest surviving example of literature in their tongue, even if it was originally composed here in Edinburgh. Scotland has many remnants of Arthurian legend that have survived the change of language that happened when Scots replaced all the P-Celtic dialects, a thousand years ago and more. And we should remember that the mention of Arthur in 'The Gododdin' is the earliest known reference to him.

This survival of a tale rooted in ancient oral tradition suggests a continuity of culture with the very distant past, as if the hill itself was some kind of communal memory store. The proof of such continuity can be seen in Wilson's report of a conversation between an old monk living out his years at Holyrood Abbey and one of the new Protestant ministers at the time of Mary Queen of Scots (*Reminiscences of Old Edinburgh* v2 p202). They were discussing the Pechs, or Picts as we now call them, the indigenous name most likely used by the Romans for all of the tribal peoples north of Hadrian's Wall, and how they had supposedly disappeared.

The old monk said, 'The Pechs ! — they're just awa wi King Arthur. They biggit (built) Samson's Ribs and the pillar-rocks on which St Anthony's Chapel stands; and when their wark was dune, they just gaed awa under the hill.'

'What hill?', responded the chaplain.

'Why, Arthur's Seat, to be sure, and whan Arthur comes back again he'll hae aw the lave (rest) o the Pechs at his tail.'

It may be worth recalling that according to Chamber's Domestic annals of Scotland, the hills to the south west of Arthur's Seat, the Pentland Hills, were still being called the Pichtland Hills in the 17th century.

This is a story told here of Arthur, just as it is told of the hero Finn MacCoul in other parts of Scotland where Gaelic, a different branch of the Celtic language was (and in some places still is) spoken. And in this idea we see much of the true magic of this place. Some scholars have suggested that in such tales we see memories of truly ancient traditions, where the very bones of the ancestors were brought forth from chambered cairns to be used in rites that sought to ensure the survival of the community through the blessing of seeds and crops, rites that have been central to human societies over vast stretches of time.

An old name for Arthur's Seat is Craggenmarf, which may be related to the Gaelic *Creag nan Marbh*, meaning 'Hill of the Dead', or an original P-Celtic *carreagan marth*, little rock of sadness. An interesting point was recently made by William Oxenham about this in his *Welsh Origins of Scottish Place Names*. He suggested the name Arthur's Seat may have come from something like *Arthurisette* which could have been the translation of an original *Caer Art*, or Seat of Arthur. He goes on to point out that this name is very like *Catraeth*, the supposed battle site where the warriors of the Gododdin fell. Some support for this comes from the statement in the poem that some of the warriors were still hung-over from the feasting on Castle Rock before the battle. It would have been some hangover to have lasted all the way to Catterick in Yorkshire, which is the generally accepted location amongst historians. By this reading, Hill of the Dead may actually commemorate the death of the Gododdin warriors.

What is clear is that the name of the hill today, Arthur's Seat, and the survival of the story of the sleeping warriors, shows a cultural continuity with the idea of Arthur as a great heroic warrior in the

Gododdin poem. After all, people only carry on telling specific stories that mean something to them, and this was particularly true in the days before reading and writing were known. And even long after literature arrived the stories continued so that even now, when Scotland is mostly literate, stories are still told. For in telling the old stories we preserve something of the ancient, traditional respect for the ancestors that was central to life before the growth of cities and the modern world. And here in the heart of one of the modern world's finest cities, the timeless rocks and wild flora of Arthur's Seat remind us that it is from the past we all grow.

We must, however, be careful not to over-romanticise this remarkable place for, as we shall see, there are reminders of a range of mundane human activities dotted around. And sometimes the darkest sides of the human character showed themselves too.

Muschat's Cairn

As you come into Holyrood park from Meadowbank, on your right behind the wall at the side of the road is a small cairn. Cairns in Scotland are traditionally heaps of stone put up in remembrance of some event or person, and their history goes back thousands of years. This one, however, commemorates a dark event from just a few centuries ago. The seclusion of Arthur's Seat from the town has long made it a place of not only mysterious but occasionally bloody and evil acts. Back in 1720, Nichol Muschat of Boghall, a surgeon, married a Miss Hall. This was before the founding of the Faculty of Medicine at the University so we cannot be too sure what level of skill Muschat had in the saving of lives. We do know his capabilities in the opposite

direction, however, and we do know that he was well-known around the taverns of Edinburgh.

At this time the drinking habits of the citizens of Edinburgh were notorious. Judges, for instance, usually had a bottle or three to hand while they sat in judgment and no business deal was finalised without drink being taken. It seems that Nichol Muschat was what we would now call a real party animal. Within three weeks of marrying the poor lass he decided the marriage had been a mistake and he began to plan ways of getting rid of his wife.

At his eventual trial it came out that he had at first offered a pair of local thugs 20 guineas to murder Mrs Muschat in Dickson's Close on the Royal Mile, but it seems he realised this might be a little too obvious. His next step was to discuss the matter with one of his regular drinking partners, Campbell of Burnbank, and they decided to get rid of her in a more peaceful way. Now Campbell was a man of some standing, being the storekeeper at Edinburgh Castle, but he was deeply in debt. On the promise of 900 guineas, a very large sum of money back then, he agreed to manufacture evidence that would allow Muschat to divorce his wife. This would have had to be evidence of adultery. As it was, this plan also failed.

By this point, it appears Muschat was beginning to obsess about the murder. He confided in his brother, James, and asked if he and his wife could assist him with his wicked endeavour. Now James was relatively poor and it is safe to assume that Muschat offered to pay him a fee if he carried out the deed. The job he and his wife were given was to poison Nichol's wife. However this pair of plotters appears to have been as useless as Campbell had shown himself to be, and despite several attempts to poison the poor woman, nothing happened. Throughout this time there was no evidence to show that Mrs Muschat was aware

of any of these goings on, and it seems she was the very model
of a dutiful wife.

At last Muschat, entirely fixated by the need to be rid of his young
wife, took her for a walk to Duddingston one evening. They went along
the path that was then known as the Duke's Walk, which followed the
line of the current road passing by St Margaret's Loch. In his coat
pocket Muschat had a large knife, which he had borrowed. At his trial
he said he had no real idea of why he had the knife. That may be taken
with a pinch of salt as during the walk, noticing that there was nobody
about, he whipped out the knife and attacked his wife. Despite her
frenzied struggles and cries for help, he overpowered her and slit her
throat, leaving the bloody body lying on the path.

Muschat then ran off to his brother's house. There he seemed to go into
some kind of depression and would not speak, but just sat looking into
the fire. Come the morning, the body was discovered and it was only a
matter of time before Muschat was arrested. He was tried and there
was no doubt of his culpability. Consequently, all of the various plots
came out and Campbell of Burnbank was dismissed from his post and
sent into exile. After all, he had nothing to do with the actual murder.
Muschat himself was sentenced to death and hanged on 6 January 1721
in the Grassmarket.

This sorry tale roused the sympathies of the public and a subscription
was raised to have a cairn built as a permanent reminder of Mrs
Muschat and the dreadful fate she had suffered. The original cairn was
raised where her body was found but over the years it has been moved
at least twice to allow for greater access to the Park.

The Wells

On approaching the great central bowl of the park that contains Hunter's Bog from Holyrood, you have to pass by a stone structure built into the side of the hill beside the road. This is St Margaret's Well which was moved here in 1859 from its previous location further east. The well was moved, stone-by-stone, to allow the North British Railway Company Workshops at Jock's Lodge to be extended. The workshops were later replaced by St Margaret's House and the original site of the well is marked by a monument in the form of a boulder. Above St Margaret's Well, there is a depression in the hillside where there used to be another well dedicated to St David. Wells, of course, have long been the sites of ritual activities. With water commonly understood as the source of all life, it is easy to see how these rituals and beliefs came about. It is an undeniable fact that many places considered sacred in pre-Christian times had wells associated with them. Many of these wells soon became associated with the Christian saints, following the recognized tradition of new religions absorbing as much as they could of whatever beliefs were prevalent before them. And Arthur's Seat was one such place, with a range of different wells.

This intriguing building is modelled on the ancient well of St Triduana at nearby Restalrig. St Triduana is one of those tantalisingly sketchy early Christian saints who seem to hearken back to the days before Christian priests walked this island. She is said to have torn out her own eyes to discourage a suitor so she could devote her life to God. She certainly succeeded. Like many of the other early saints, Triduana, whose various Scottish wells were long associated with rituals designed to heal eye problems, gives us a link back to the culture that had grown up over many millennia in Scotland among the peoples who came here after the last Ice Age.

If you look through the grille into the room that houses the spring, you will see a variety of coins. These have been placed here by visitors carrying on the belief that the spirit associated with the well must be given respect. In more modern terms, the coins have been thrown in for good luck. Often small rags of cloth were hung on nearby trees as a form of sympathetic magic. The rags represented ailments or infirmities, which could be of the mind or heart as well as the body. As the rags wore away, it was thought that the affliction itself would disappear. People still do this and there are several such wells in Scotland, the most famous being the Cloutie Well, near Avoch on the Black Isle just north of Inverness.

While the glaciers of the last Ice Age scarred much of Scotland's landscape, Arthur's Seat is much, much older than that. The hill that soars above St Margaret's Well is a volcanic plug that has been described as 'the finest example of a small extinct volcano to be found anywhere'. Several books have been written about the geology of this place, and its role in the development of modern geology is well documented.

Haggis Knowe

As you go past the well and head towards Hunter's Bog, the central depression in the massif of the hill, to your left there is a small knoll. This is Haggis Knowe, which most commentators have interpreted as being from the Scots Haggs, meaning broken ground, and Knowe, a small hill. However, it is not entirely clear where the broken ground refers to. Certainly the land here must have changed considerably over the centuries, given the ongoing human activity in the area, and perhaps this place was particularly rough. However, there is another interpretation.

Given the repeated suggestions of ritual activities taking place on and around Arthur's Seat, another interpretation might well be Hag's Knowe. Hag, of course, means an old woman and is often linked with the idea of the witch. However, in ancient Scottish lore, amongst both Scots and Gaelic speakers, the Hag is something more. She is the Cailleach or Carlin, the almost demonic spirit of Winter who was said to have created much of our landscape, including North Berwick Law which is visible from many parts of Arthur's Seat. With her control over the weather and her power to bring the dead back to life, she can be seen as having been at one time a version of the mother Goddess herself. And if this mini-mountain was the site of ritual practice in the far past, we may well expect there to be some reference to the being that represented the very life-force that kept the season turning and all life reseeding itself. Perhaps we can never know but it is always interesting to speculate.

St Anthony's Well and The Fairy Knowe

As we skirt the western edge of Haggis Knowe, we are faced with yet another reminder of ancient sanctity. Slightly to the left and up a small incline lies a massive boulder with a stone carved basin at its foot. This is St Anthony's Well, probably another ancient water source that had its name changed as the dominant belief system of the inhabitants developed into Christianity. And up to the left, looming over the well, are the remains of St Anthony's Chapel. This can be seen nestling into a cliff face on the side of Whinny Hill which used to be known as Fairy Knowe. This was certainly a healing well, and the spring which fed it is said to have originally been further up the hill towards the Chapel. The belief in these wells' healing powers has retained something of a hold on the human imagination, as mentioned previously. This is an eyewitness account from the Proceedings of the Society of Antiquaries of Scotland for 1882–83,

> 'While walking in the Queen's Park about sunset, I casually passed St Anthony's Well, and had my attention attracted by the number of people about it, all simply quenching their thirst, some probably with a dim idea that they would reap some benefit from the draught. Standing a little apart, however, and evidently patiently waiting a favourable moment to present itself for their purpose, was a group of four. Feeling somewhat curious as to their intention I quietly kept myself in the background, and by-and-by was rewarded. The crowd departed and the group came forward, consisting of two old women, a younger woman of about 30, and a pale, sickly-looking girl—a child three or four years old. Producing cups from their pockets, the old women dipped them in the pool, filled them, and drank the contents. A full cup was then presented to the younger woman and another to the child. Then one of the old women produced a long linen bandage, dipped it in the water, wrung it, dipped it in again, and then wound it round the child's head, covering the eyes. The youngest woman, evidently the mother of the child, carefully observed the operation, weeping gently all the time. The other old woman, not engaged in this work, was carefully filling a clear glass bottle with the water, evidently for future use. Then, after the principal operators had looked at each other with an earnest and half solemn sort of look, the party wended its way down the hill.'

And it seems certain that some of the familiar visitors to Arthur's Seat on Beltane morning used to visit this well. Various reports over the years, some from the 20th century, have mentioned whole crowds of local people coming to Arthur's Seat on May morning, often in processions led by pipers. As mentioned already, in recent years several of Scotland's ancient healing wells have seen renewed activity and, just as in the visit to St Anthony's Well, they reflect at least remnants of an ongoing continuity with the past that answers some kind of need in people.

And just who was St Anthony? He seems to have been a fourth century Egyptian saint to whom the chapel here was dedicated. We know that it was the practice of the early Christians to locate their church on sites that were already believed to be sacred. Was this such a site? It certainly seems possible and the late Australian poet Alexander Hope put forward an intriguing suggestion in his stimulating book, *A Midsummer Eve's Dream*. In this he analyses the 15th century Scots poet Robert Henryson's work the *Tretis of The Tua Mariit Wemen and the Wedo* (The Treatise of the Two Married Women and the Widow). He sees the poem, which has the three women meeting and discussing various aspects of life – particularly men folk – as being a thinly veiled reference to what he saw as a Fairy Cult still existing in Henryson's time. He goes so far as to suggest that the bower in which these three women met was situated somewhere on Arthur's Seat. The chapel, the ruin of which has the look of a Victorian folly, is of course authentic, though the earliest reference to it is no earlier than the 15th century.

Close by on the rock scarp called the Dasses, which overlooks the Volunteers Walk leading into the centre of the park, there is another reminder of past practices. The great folklorist Donald Mackenzie mentioned that in the late 19th century children used to slide down what were known as the Slidey Stanes, which he thought was a remnant of an old fertility rite where women would slide down the rock to ensure success in either falling pregnant or in having an easy birth. On the outcrop, part of the rock face is smoother than the rest. At the top of the rock is carved a simple cross. This may well have been a way of 'de-paganising' the site, probably at the time of the Reformation but possibly much earlier.

To the Hill
Symphony for Holyrood
Three
scherzo

Sidestep in time
history's dance
on Arthur's Seat
beacons blaze
the fabled king
rides south to war
shieldwall Saxon
bloodied red
before day's dawn
Celtic lament
at Tref-yr-Lyn
swords in the lake
between deershorns
sign of the cross
Margaret's relics
Haly Rude
sair sanct for the crown
David's gift
Kingdom of Scots
siege perilous
Scots wha hae
Bannockburn
Royal Hunting Park

Stewart dynasty
Reine de France
Queen of Scots
Thrie Estaites
John Commonweill
move up Jock
Jamie the Saxt
gie us a break
civil wars
gang tae the muir
gallows tree
Act of Union
parcel o rogues
the Stuart's return
redcoat walls
hey Johnnie Cope
Charlie's awa
British Empire
radical road
Regina Vic
Tartan trews
war memorial
hill of the dead
begin again
Holyrood.

Camstane Quarry

As you head into the park towards Hunter's Bog with the Dasses to your left, and behind them the rock face called the Lang Rig, the ground rises up to your right towards the top of the Salisbury Crags which look out west over St Leonard's. The name Salisbury may well come from an old Anglian term Salis, meaning willow. On this side of the crags there are deep pits in the hillside marking the old Camstane quarry. As far back as the creation of the Abbey of Holyrood in the 12th century, sandstone was taken from here and also from along the rock face of Salisbury Crags. This quarrying went on into the 19th century and herein lies another tale.

It concerns the Earl of Haddington in the 1820s. We can perhaps gather something of his character from the fact that he was taken to court in 1824 over his refusal to pay his contribution to the poor rates in the Canongate parish. He owed this because of his hereditary position as Keeper of the King's Park, a position his family had initially held back in the time of King James VI. Previous to this, Haddington had resisted the idea of opening up Arthur's Seat by creating paths and installing seats, an idea which had been put forward by a local society to encourage the study of botany. This was part of the widespread interest in the physical sciences which sprang up during the Enlightenment. The group concerned also wanted to plant exotic imported plants and flowers in the park. He refused to even consider it as he said it would be an infringement of the rights of his tenant who grazed sheep there.

But it was his apparent greed in another matter that led to Haddington's family losing their role as Keepers of the King's Park, The case was a great scandal in the 1820s and the papers of the time followed it in great detail. It seems that the Earl was extracting a great deal of stone from the Camstane quarry to help in the building of Edinburgh's New Town. Although the quarries here had been used in earlier centuries, it seems the Earl saw a particular opportunity in re-opening them. Not only did it supply much of the material for the extension of the New Town but he was also selling stone for paving London's streets, extracting as much as a hundred tons a day. This was too much for some of Edinburgh's citizenry, who began writing to the local papers to complain about the despoliation of a noted beauty spot. This, in fact, seems to have been the very first time a campaign was started to protect a scenic part of the environment against commercial exploitation, something we are now well used to.

The Earl was in no way minded to pay attention to such protests and carried on quarrying. This, of course, only increased the feelings of anger towards him. One prominent opponent of his actions was Lady Gwydyr who decided to go direct to the King, George IV, and complain about the desecration of what was, after all, the King's Park. This brought matters to a head and in a hearing in the House of Lords in 1831, the new Earl of Haddington, who had recently succeeded his late father, was stripped of his hereditary rights as Keeper of the King's Park. However, he was awarded the sum of £40,000 as compensation for his trouble. Salisbury Crags were saved but at considerable cost to the public purse.

The Crags

The Salisbury Crags themselves have what can only be described as a chequered past. Like the summit of Arthur's Seat, they can be seen from miles away, being clearly visible from various parts of Fife on the north side of the river. They were the site of various duels in the 16th and

17th centuries. Being separate from the town, they provided a suitable spot for settling matters with the sword, not an uncommon occurrence in Scottish history, and many of the Highland clans continued to carry weapons right up to the Disarming Act of 1746. This is the act that also outlawed the wearing of kilts and the playing of bagpipes, except for members of the British Army. The participants in the fights, reported as happening on and around Arthur's Seat, seem to have come from all walks of life and are occasionally a bit surprising. And the fights don't always seem to have been fair. John Knox, generally known as the father of the Scottish Reformation, had a close colleague, John Craig, who was by his side during the momentous years around 1660. Craig had a son by the name of John Brand, who is reported to have stabbed William King, a fellow student at the College of Philosophy of Edinburgh, at the Crags in the 1660s. He was beheaded.

The Crags were the scene of a particularly unfortunate incident in 1770. An Excise Officer, Mungo Campbell, had been imprisoned in the Tolbooth awaiting execution for the killing of the Earl of Eglinton in a dispute over poaching on the Earl's lands in Ayrshire. The day after he was sentenced, Campbell committed suicide. While handing down the sentence, the judge had further decreed that his body be handed over to the Faculty of Anatomy for medical dissection.

The anatomists of Edinburgh were notoriously keen to get their hands on corpses to further their medical investigations at this time, and were not too particular about where the bodies were coming from. Campbell's counsel at the trial objected that this was not within the powers of the judge to order, so after the execution by hanging, the body was handed over to Campbell's family and friends. As a suicide, his body was barred from being buried in consecrated ground so a private burial was arranged at the foot of Salisbury Crags.

However, the funeral party was watched by local people and soon the Edinburgh mob gathered. In a strange reversal of their normal attitudes, which were generally to support those who broke the law, the mob had built up resentment at Campbell for the killing of Eglinton. Once the mourners had left, they arrived at the grave, dug up the body and proceeded to throw it about. They ended up carrying it to the top of the cliffs and throwing it over. Campbell's distressed friends re-gathered the now smashed up body and, to prevent further indignities, hired a boat and buried him out in the Firth of Forth.

And, of course, the isolation of this part of Arthur's Seat made it attractive to a specific part of Edinburgh society; smugglers and criminals. Now smuggling is often thought of as the importing of goods from abroad to avoid tax. What it actually means is the avoidance of paying tax on goods, and in Scotland this applied to illicit whisky. There are no records of anyone having had a still on Arthur's Seat, but an interesting discovery was made in 1728 on the westernmost point of the Crags, which may have had something to do with smuggling, or certainly some kind of criminality. Half way up the cleft known as the Cat Nick, the climbing of which was rite of passage for local teenagers for centuries, a cave was found. It was described as a 'snug little room, with a lamp hanging from the roof, and lighted by a little window covered with a bladder'. Supposedly it had been the den of a hermit in ancient times, but later became the 'den of a gang of thieves'. The use of a bladder hints at whisky smuggling, as it was in animal bladders that the peatreekers – so known for their smoke-dark complexions created by tending their stills in enclosed spaces – used to bring the *uisge beatha* (whisky) into the towns. The bladders could be hidden in all sorts of places, including under clothes and particularly within the undergarments of women! Whether there had ever been an ancient hermit here is unclear, but even in the 18th century this was an isolated spot.

Like Muschat's Cairn, the Salisbury Crags also have their share of events of a darker character. Just below the end of the Crags, where the path comes up from Hunter's Bog through the gap known as the Hause, is the outcrop known as Echo Rock, from where a resounding echo was reputed to be heard to any shout. Looking up at the summit to the left is the quaintly named Guttit Haddie. This scree slope in the side of the hill is so named for its resemblance to a gutted haddock and was caused by a spectacular torrent of rainwater in 1724. If you follow the low road round the edge of the hill you pass below Samson's Ribs, a notable geological feature of five sided greenstone columns on the hillside which are about 60 feet high. A little further on another part of the cliff has long been known as Hangman's Craig. It too has a story. Back in the reign of Charles II, the local hangman was a man from the Borders. Hangmen were always seen as pariahs and were generally unpopular with all walks of life. This particular man had been born into money but had fallen on hard times due to a fondness for the good things in life, and his reduced circumstances had led to him taking on the position of executioner. However, he tried to make the best of things and regularly mixed with what he considered the better class of person around the town. At this point, golf was popular and he liked to join the crowds on Bruntsfield Links, where the sport was regularly played. However, one day he was recognised by some golfers who had recently lost a friend at his hands, and they turned on him. The Borderer ran off, pursued by threats and curses. It shook him to the core. The very next day the extent of his reaction to this public humiliation was only too clear. His body was found at the bottom of this section of the cliff face, which was then given the name of Hangman's Rock.

Murder Acre

Back in 1677, the Edinburgh magistrates decided to hold a parade
in honour of the birthday of King Charles II on 29 June. At first the
intention was to have 16 companies of trained bands, the local
militia, plus one company each representing the merchants and trades
made up of young men. The plan was to stage a Wappenschaw,
a long-established Scottish custom dating from before the 1603 Union
of the Crowns, when the men of a particular area were called out to
present themselves with whatever weapons they had. This was simply
to ensure that the populace was prepared to defend itself against any
invasion from England, something that had happened all too often in
the bloody history between the two countries.

There was, however, some tension around this particular muster as
there was bad blood between the young men of the Merchants
Association and those of the Trades Association, who made up their
respective armed groups. No one knows what sparked it off, but for
the sake of public safety the magistrates decided that although all the
trained bands could march, it would be better if only one of the other
two companies turned up for the parade. The Merchants were chosen
and the young men of the Trades Association were informed that their
presence wasn't welcome on the day, though they would be given the
opportunity to parade at a later, unspecified, date.

This decision did not go down well with the young Trades lads. As the
day approached, there was a great deal of discussion and outright
dissent on the streets of Edinburgh, with the general population clearly
on the side of the Trades. At this time, Edinburgh had long had a
tradition of rioting. In the days before there was even a semblance
of democracy, the only chance that the common people had of having
their voices heard was to riot. Taking to the streets and refusing to obey

the rule of law, such as it was, had a long and very well established history in Edinburgh. As the fateful day approached, feelings were running high. The days leading up to the Saturday appointed for the parade saw regular skirmishes between the young men of the Trades Association and members of the Town Guard. These had resulted in six of the former being arrested and put in the Tolbooth, the town jail.

The arrests only served to increase the tension and, on the Saturday, a crowd of between 1,500 and 2,000 gathered below Echo Rock, on the south west corner of Arthur's Seat. There was great deal of tension in the air. As it happens, even today, whenever those in power feel themselves affronted by people refusing to do as they are told, the situation rapidly escalates. The Magistrates, inflamed at the insolence of the mob, sent two of the Baillies to order them to disperse. Rather than do so, the mob simply took the Baillies prisoner, sending word to the rest of the Magistrates that they would be released as soon as the six men in the Tolbooth were set free.

This was too much for the dignity of the magistrates to bear. At once they sent for Major Cockburne of the King's Troops to disperse the crowd at Echo Rock. The major went to confront the crowd with his dragoons; thirty mounted professional soldiers armed with swords and firearms. They were well trained in the use of their weapons and though the magistrates had hoped that a few rounds fired over the heads of the crowd would be enough to disperse them, it did not turn out that way.

As the dragoons rode towards the crowd with their firearms at the ready, a woman sitting on a nearby dyke shouted out that they only had powder in their guns. This was not the case, as she found out to her cost. She had barely got the words out when one of the dragoons fired at her. The bullet passed through her lower body and she fell

from the dyke in a bloody heap, to die a few days later. Seeing this, the crowd, angry but unarmed, turned and started to flee towards Duddingston. Here, in the fields just west of the loch, the dragoons began firing into the fleeing crowd. Several young men died there, shot in the back. From then on, the people of Edinburgh and Duddingston called the place Murder Acre, for murder surely had been done. No warning was given, no warning shots fired, just the simple exercise of physical force to uphold the magistrate's idea of power.

The Risings

The wildness of the Crags was eventually tamed by putting a path in along the bottom of the cliff face. This is known as the Radical Road and opinions vary as to how it got its name. Some think it was created by out of work weavers from the west of Scotland who were paid by Sir Walter Scott and his friends to put the road in. Others reckon that these weavers were doing hard labour for their part in the Rising of 1820, where calls for political and economic reform amongst Lanarkshire weavers were stage-managed by government agents into a pathetic attempt at an armed rising.

There is a record of unemployed weavers being hired by the Superintendent of Public Works in 1820, but this was to level ground below the North Bridge and at London Street. Given Sir Walter's absolute loyalty to the Crown and his son-in-law's active participation on the local Yeomanry Regiment (used to keep the common people down on various occasions), the latter might be closer to the truth. Thus far it is a bit of a mystery, one which has been echoed in more modern times by the changing of the name of a nearby pub from The Right Wing to The Radical Road!

On 17 September 1745, Prince Charles Edward Stewart, who has gone down in history as Bonnie Prince Charlie, arrived from the north-west with an army of over 5,000 men. He was intent on taking back the throne of Great Britain for his father James VIII of Scotland and II of England.

Approaching Edinburgh from the west, the Prince's army, which at this point was mainly composed of Highlanders, came to the south side of Arthur's Seat to set up camp. At first, they marched into the area of Hunter's Bog through the Hause. Leaving most of his troops there, Prince Charles rode forward to the ground below St Anthony's chapel where, for the first time, he looked down on Holyrood Palace, the home of his ancestors. Heading towards the Palace, he passed the very spot where his great-great-great-great grandmother, the tragic Mary Queen of Scots, held a great banquet in 1564, in celebration of the marriage of Lord and Lady Fleming. This seems to have been some-where in the dip now known as the Dry Dam.

A great crowd had gathered, many of them supporters of the Jacobite Rising and others simply there out of curiosity. As Charlie came into the palace there was cheering from the crowd, and over the next few weeks his presence in the capital was the cause of much celebration. While there were a series of balls in his honour, those who were loyal supporters of the Hanoverian government of the time simply kept quiet.

Initially the Prince had about a thousand of his men around him at Holyrood, while the rest of them were split between Hunter's Bog and the high ground above Duddingston. The brightly coloured tartans of the Highland troops must have made a grand sight amidst the lofty grandeur of the Seat. No doubt there were sentries on the very top of Arthur's Seat keeping a look out for approaching troops and for any sign of ships of the Royal Navy coming up the Firth of Forth.

After the famous victory of Prestonpans on 21 September, the Jacobite army returned but this time encamped at the foot of Arthur's Seat on the south side, to the west of Duddingston village. Just over six months later this army was shattered on the field of Culloden, near Inverness, after a series of military blunders. Though Highlanders, loyal to the Jacobite cause, fought a low-level guerrilla campaign in the Highlands until the mid-1750s, after this the Jacobite Risings in Scotland were effectively over.

Something which may be a macabre memento of the Prince's short stay was discovered in 1828, during the excavations for the building of the Innocent Railway which ran through the south-western corner of Holyrood Park. Three skeletons were found, three feet below the surface. Alongside the bones was a large dirk, the ubiquitous weapon of the Highlander. This led to speculation that these may have been the mortal remains of three Jacobites who had fallen out with some of their comrades.

The railway, the tunnel of which is now a cycle and footpath was, according to some, called the Innocent Railway because, unlike many other early railways, it never had a casualty in its building or during its operation. Another explanation is that it was a horse drawn railway from its opening in 1831 till 1845, and as such it was a gentler and much less dangerous method of travel than its steam counterpart.

Dunsapie

As one climbs higher up Arthur's Seat, the views expand out over the Firth of Forth, Fife and beyond to the north and out to the west. Before reaching the summit, however, we should briefly consider Dunsapie Craig, the lesser hill to the south. Here, there are ancient remnants of cultivation terraces, settlements and a walled area, thought to have been a fort.

There is something on the south eastern close of Dunsapie Craig which again may take us back to the ritual behaviour that has so marked the long human interaction with Arthur's Seat as a whole. Here there is a very large, roundish boulder resting on a bed of rock. It is tempting to see this as a remnant of a Logan stone. These were reckoned to be 'druidical remains' in bygone days in Britain, but similar rocks have been found all over the world. These were massive boulders, so balanced on bedrock that they can be moved by a gentle push. They would then gently rock which gave them their other name of Rocking Stones. The tradition in Scotland is that they were the sites of courts of justice in times long gone, and that the rocking of the stones was used as form of judgement. They occur both naturally and in man-made form and there are records of them being knocked over by pious Christians, intent on removing sites and symbols of 'paganism'.

As you head up towards the actual summit of the hill, there are lines across the slope which are believed to be the remnants of cultivation terraces. This underlines the interaction people have always had with this place, even if today such activity is mostly recreational or tourist-driven. The work of the staff of Holyrood Park in maintaining the path to ensure the safety of visitors is exemplary, but even to this day this can be a dangerous place, particularly when the rock is wet, and care must always be taken.

The Wild Macraas

On the main summit there are remains of an enclosing wall which may have been a fort. However, like many other hill-top sites, people in the far past had a range of uses for them apart from military ones. There is nevertheless one military event that took place here that is much more recent than any Dark Age or Iron Age warrior band.

Here on the summit of Arthur's Seat and on Nether Hill immediately to the south, a remarkable event took place towards the end of the 18th century. A regiment of Seaforth Highlanders, raised as a Fencible Regiment in the Highlands, had been brought in to Edinburgh Castle. Fencible Regiments were specifically raised for the defence of the realm in the ongoing war with the French, and on being recruited into them, men were told that they would not have to serve abroad.

In the period after the failed Jacobite rising of 1745, as the ancient tribal system of the Highland Clans was eradicated in often bloody scenes, there was little opportunity for employment and the Highland regiments of the British army filled up with young men desperate to earn a living. Coming from the martial background of Highland society, soldiering was always an option but most of them did not want to go abroad with the army. In 1778, the regiment numbering 1,300 men from the traditional MacKenzie lands of Wester Ross took over the garrisoning of Edinburgh Castle. Among them were many of the sub-clan, or sept, the Macraes, long known as the Wild Macraas, and they were soon to live up to their reputation.

On 5 August, word came that there was to be an attempted invasion by French troops near Greenock on the west coast, so several hundred of the Seaforths were sent to resist this. As so often in the 18th century, Britain and France were at war, fighting to control much of the world's trade as the western empires stretched out over the whole globe. It was a false alarm, but when the detachments returned to the castle it was to find that Leith harbour was full of transport ships sent to convoy them off to foreign service.

A rumour spread that they would only be going to the Channel Islands but many of the men, particularly the Macraes, were disinclined to believe that. Their officers would tell them nothing. They were soldiers in the King's Army now and their duty was simply to do as they were told. It was as if the idea of the Fencible Regiments had never existed. Soon the word was being passed that they were in fact to be sent to India. The position of the command appears to have been that these simple Highlanders could be ordered about at will and that they would end up doing what they were told, notwithstanding the promises made on their recruitment. It did not quite work out like that.

On the day set for embarkation, 22 September, as the regiment reluctantly headed for the port, 400 of them, muskets loaded and with two tartan plaids as banners and pipers playing, marched off separately. They went through the town and tried to head off their companions on their way to the ships, but after brief skirmish in which several men were wounded, they fell back.

Then, cheered on by many of the locals who were enjoying the spectacle and who sympathised with their cause, the contingent marched in ranks right to the top of Arthur's Seat. There they threw up a redoubt, a wall from behind which they would have cover if they had to open fire, set sentinels, and went to sleep. The Army High Command at the castle were in a frenzy. This was blatant mutiny. Word was sent to various troops and by the next day a force of nearly 1,000 men, infantry and dragoons, arrived in the city ready to storm the camp on Arthur's Seat.

At this stage however, sanity prevailed and three senior officers, The Earl of Dunmore, Lord MacDonald and General Oughton, ascended the hill to talk to the Macraes and MacKenzies. They listened to what the men had to say about their fears that they were being sold into slavery by their officers. After some negotiations involving the immediate settlement of outstanding pay, always a matter of dispute in the army in those days, the recalcitrant Highlanders agreed to accept their orders. The result was that on the 29 September they all embarked on the ships that ironically were to take them to Guernsey, but only for a short stop, before sailing onto India. Their reluctance to accept being sent abroad proved to have been eminently sensible, for almost a quarter of them died on the long sea-journey to India and only around 400 of them were fit enough to go into action in April 1782.

All in all, this was a tragic incident that demonstrates only too clearly the expendability of Highland troops as far as the High Command of the British Army was concerned. So what if they had been promised not to be sent abroad; they were barely more than savages and what did their ideas matter? Given the association of Arthur's Seat with the great hero Arthur and the courageous warriors of the Gododdin, this story is a rather sad epitaph for the military history of the place.

On The Summit

The top of Arthur's Seat is a striking place. Like many of Scotland's higher mountains, it can often be shrouded in mist and, despite living only a mile away, it is often invisible from my window. But like all Scots, I am well acclimatised to the vagaries of our weather. We can only hope that it was a sunny day in 1661 when there was a race from the Figgate Burn in Portobello to the top of Arthur's Seat. The prize for the winner was a hundred pound cheese, with a bottle of whisky and another of rum for the runner-up, a term well deserved in this instance! Those women must have been fit.

There is a specific sense of place up on the summit. Cultures throughout history and all over the world have constantly seen hill and mountain tops as being in some way magical, sacred places. The idea of the sleeping warriors somewhere inside the hill itself is surely a part of this. These sleeping warriors, to some extent, represent the ancestors of those who told and continue to tell their story. Until relatively recently, most people in the world lucky enough to live in the same locale for succeeding generations always had a sense of respect for their ancestors. This is not necessarily ancestor worship as such, more a sense of respect and honour given to previous members of one's common family and community who had laid the basis for contemporary society.

This is a common human idea, and the concept of attachment to the land is one which is central to growing issues of environmentalism and sustainability in our fast-changing modern world. And just as Edinburgh, the capital of Scotland, is in many ways at the heart of the nation, so Arthur's Seat is, in some special sense, at the very heart of the idea of Edinburgh.

Edinburgh is famed throughout the world for its cultural extravaganza of Festivals; famous, also, for setting the model for so many modern cities with its New Town arising from its role at the centre of the 18th century Enlightenment, which ushered in the modern world as we know it. Edinburgh is an international centre of commerce and finance, the home of Scots Law, and the home of a new Parliament which many of us hope soon to see leading an independent country once again into the family of nations. But there is more to life than money, more to life than the law, more to life than politics. And Arthur's Seat reminds us of that. Here, in the very heart of a modern city looking to the future, is a place of wildness, of ancient sanctity and a place that reminds us that although we can control our environment to some extent, we cannot master it.

And in that awareness, as you look out from the summit of Arthur's Seat, other places and ideas come into view. For here, perched above the great river, we see out and beyond into the Scottish landscape. And it is fortuitous, if nothing more, that so many places we can see from here likewise remind us of Scotland's history and prehistory. Nearby is Calton Hill, where the medieval Robin Hood Games took place annually with their Abbot of Unreason and their temporary role reversal of rich and poor linked to the Beltane ceremonies. These ceremonies have been reborn and refashioned in recent times so that the Beltane fires of renewal and rebirth can reach out once again over the landscape.

There is the great rock of Edinburgh Castle, *Castello Puellarum* (the Castle of the Maidens) as it was once known, part of the same volcano that once belched here where the warriors of the Gododdin feasted for whole year before setting our on their heroic and final battle. And beyond there are so many more significant landmarks.

Off to the east is the massif of Traprain Law where St Kentigern's mother Thenew, or Tennoch, miraculously survived attempted execution by her father, King Lot of the Lothians. North of it stands North Berwick Law, one of the Paps of Lothian. Like Arthur's Seat itself, this was said to have been made by the Carlin, the ancient goddess, in a strikingly fundamental way – when farting. North Berwick is also the place where a coven of local witches allegedly strove to bring abut the death of James vi in the 1590s.

Then further north out in the Firth of Forth, the Isle of May – the island of the maidens – can be seen on some days and in some weathers. This often mist-enshrouded island was probably the Avalon of Arthurian legend, to which the dying king was taken by Morgan and her eight sisters in the local version of the story. So the May was a place of pilgrimage even before the monks arrived there. It could also have been the home of the great Warrior-woman Scathach, who gave arms to the Ulster hero Cuchullain in Irish tradition.

Further to the north, on the Fife coast, stands Largo Law where a local saint struggled with the Devil. And beyond it on clear days, looking over the town of Kirkcaldy, you can see the Sidlaws (sometimes called the Seedlies, the Hills of the Sidh or the Fairies) that run along the north bank of the Tay. Beyond them, particularly when the snow is lying, you can see the Braes and Glens of Angus above Dundee, and occasionally the outline of the great massif of Lochnagar. This great mountain, too, has its memories of the ancient Cailleach, the Gaelic equivalent of the Carlin, and its own paps, or breast-shaped hills.

Coming further west and much closer we see the Paps of Fife, East and West Lomond Hill, with their ancient monuments, wells, Maiden Castle and other remnants of ancient beliefs and rituals of fertility. In one such story, there is the turning of the local witch Carlin Maggie into a pillar of stone after she dared to take on the Devil himself in a contest of magic. Between Edinburgh and those hills you can make out the Sleeping Giant on the south side of Loch Leven, that some see as a recumbent female form in the landscape. Others, thinking of the hill's name, Benarty, and its link with Arthur, consider it to be a warrior in the landscape.

Further to the west, at the end of the Ochil Hills and towards the ancient town of Stirling with its Round Table below the castle, is the peak of Dumyat, linked to that other early Scottish tribe the Maetae. And just past that rounded peak is the soaring mountain of Ben Ledi, which some have translated as the Hill of God. It is certainly a place where the fires of Beltane used to be lit and has on its summit, *Cnoc a Cailleach*, the knoll of the Cailleach.

Following these ranges even further to the west you reach Ben Lomond, whose name, like those of the Paps of Fife, also takes us back to Beltane as the name means fire or beacon hill. On clear days beyond them all you see the Grampian Hills, the great mountain range of Scotland, stretching all the way north to Inverness. If the weather is clear, looking northwest over the ridge at the east end of the Ochil Hills, just as they slope towards their high point, there is the tip of a far away mountain jutting over the line of the hills. This is Schiehallion, a name translated as the Fairy Hill of the Caledonians, another early tribal name the Romans used, and another place with links to the Old Cailleach. Sixty miles away from Arthur's Seat, there is no problem in seeing this ancient sacred mountain on clear days, especially when clad with snow in winter. It is as if this line of sight to the mountain in the heart of the city is a visceral link, reminding us that no matter how far we think we are from nature, she is there beside us at all times.

And of course, through time, the Goddess has had her consort, and here that consort was surely Arthur. However nebulous a figure, he was clearly deep-rooted in the culture of the people living here in the First Millennium. Was he a giant, a god, a hero? We may never know, but over the years many things have been said of him. The great Scottish ethnologist Lewis Spence, like others before him, saw a link between Arthur and the bear, and there have been many scholars suggesting that this is the underlying meaning of his name. Bears have long been significant figures in mythology as figures of strength and knowledge, and also of child-bearing and motherhood; the ferocity of a mother bear in defending her children is famous. But the power and ferocity when aroused make the bear a truly suitable totem or guardian-spirit for warriors and chiefs. It has also been noted that any of the sites associated with Arthur in Britain have alignments that point due north; north to the Pole Star, part of Ursa Major, the Great Bear constellation. And of course Arthur, like Etin, has come down in many instances as a giant. And in the Etin we see links that step outside the tradition of the Celtic-speaking peoples of this land. For the Etin is rooted in Scandinavian culture, reminding us that here on the east coast of Scotland, contact with our cousins over the sea in Denmark, Norway and beyond, started not long after the Ice Age passed and has never stopped. And while linguists may protest, our ears tell us that there is at least the possibility that Etin survives today in our city's very name.

Truly, on Arthur's Seat, with its pre-Christian and Christian sites of sanctity and ritual, we can find a way to be in touch with the planet that sustains us all. There have been many alterations to Arthur's Seat; both St Margaret's Loch and Dunsapie Loch are artificial, roads were put in, and a few areas have been extensively drained. But the Hill retains a sense of otherness that is almost tangible. To stand at Hunter's Bog and look around you hear little, if any, city noise, and see no city streets. You could be deep in the heart of the mountains. And this sense

of place, of closeness to Mother Earth, is as strong today for local and visitor alike as it has been for countless generations of people who saw Arthur's Seat as their own special place.

Postscript

We have seen that local writers, Scott, Hogg, and more recently Rankin have utilised Arthur's Seat but they are not the only ones. Robert Louis Stevenson called it, 'a hill for magnitude, a mountain in virtue of its bold design', but it is not only Scots who have found inspiration in this atmospheric place. One of the most interesting is Jules Verne, who in his book 'The Underground City' has the character Nell. She has been raised in an underground environment and taken up Arthur's Seat at night time. She has never seen the sun. Edinburgh is called Coal City in the novel. Verne writes,

> 'The girl's eyes were therefore turned towards the east. Harry, close to her, was watching her anxiously. Would she not be too strongly impressed by these first rays of daylight? All stayed silent. Even Jack Ryan was quiet.
>
> Already a little pale line, nuanced in pink, was being drawn above the horizon on a background of light mist. A remnant of thin clouds, astray in the zenith, was attacked by the first stroke of light. At the foot of Arthur's Seat, in the absolute calm of the night a still drowsy Edinburgh hazily appeared. Some points of light pierced the darkness here and there. They were the morning stars that the people of the Old Town were lighting. Behind, in the west, the horizon, intersected by random silhouettes, marked the boundary of a region of hilly peaks, on which each sunray would place a feather of fire.

Meanwhile, the edge of the sea was becoming more clearly defined towards the east. The range of colours was gradually drawing up in the order of the solar spectrum. The red of the first mists was turning tone by tone to the violet of the zenith. With each second the palette became more intense: pink became red, red became fire. The day was forming at the point of intersection that the diurnal arc was about to make with the circumference of the sea.

At this moment, Nell's eyes were scanning from the foot of the hill to the city, where the different quarters were becoming distinguishable. Some pointed steeples emerged here and there on high monuments, and their outlines stood out more sharply. There spread a sort of ashen light. Finally, a first ray reached the girl's eye. It was the green ray, which in the evening or morning, escapes from the sea when the horizon is pure.

Half a minute later, Nell stood up and stretched her hand towards a point that dominated the area of the New Town.

'A fire!' she said.

'No, Nell,' replied Harry, 'it's not a fire. It's the golden touch of the sun on the top of the Scott Monument!'

And, indeed, the extreme tip of the pinnacle, two hundred feet high, was glowing like a superb lighthouse.

Day had come. The sun burst forth. Its disc still seemed damp, as if it had really risen from the waters of the sea. Initially stretched by refraction, it gradually shrunk to a circle. Its bright-ness, soon unbearable, was like the mouth of a furnace hollowed in the sky.

Nell immediately had to almost close her eyes. Over her too thin eyelids she still had to place her fingers, tightly closed.

Harry wanted her to turn towards the opposite horizon.

'No, Harry,' she said, 'my eyes have to get used to seeing what your eyes can see.'

Through the palm of her hands, Nell could still make out a pink glow, which whitened as the sun rose above the horizon. Her eyes gradually got used to it. Then, her eyelids opened, and her eyes finally beheld the light of day.

The pious child fell to her knees, crying:

'God, how beautiful your world is!'

The girl lowered her eyes then and looked. At her feet unfolded the panorama of Edinburgh: the new and carefully arranged areas of the New Town, the jumbled mass of houses and strange network of streets of the Old Town. Two heights dominated this ensemble: the castle, set on its basalt rock, and Calton Hill, with the modern ruins of a Greek monument on its rounded summit. Magnificent tree-lined roads radiated from the capital to the countryside. To the north, the Firth of Forth cut deeply into the coast, onto which opened the port of Leith. Above, in the distant background, lay the harmonious coast of the county of Fife. A road, straight as the road to Piraeus, linked this Athens of the North to the sea. Towards the west stretched the fine beaches of Newhaven and Portobello, whose sand tinted the first waves of the surf with yellow. In the open sea, some launches animated the waters of the firth, and two or three steamers plumed the sky with a cone of black smoke. Then, beyond, lay the vast green ocean. Modest hills dented the plain here and there. To the north, the Lomond Hills, in the west Ben Lomond and Ben Ledi reflected the solar rays, as if eternal ice had covered the peaks.

ARTHUR'S SEAT: JOURNEYS AND EVOCATIONS

Nell could not speak. Her lips only murmured vague words. Her arms were shaking. Her head was spinning with vertigo. One moment and her strength failed her. In this air so pure, before this sublime spectacle, she felt suddenly weak, and fell unconscious into Harry's waiting arms'[1]

This is a place of true inspiration, and more. For this city, with its academic and philosophic traditions, its commerce, law and governance, needs a place of wildness, a place of nature to ground it and to give it heart, and a place that, ever-changing in the always interesting Scottish climate, still inspires the native and the visitor today.

---

[1] Verne, Jules. *The Underground City*. Edinburgh: Luath Press, 2005. Print. pp.167–169.

To the Hill
Symphony for Holyrood
Four
finale, moderato

The landward light goes down
by birkie braes and broom
till sheen of water opens, wavering dusk,
ringed by trees and leafy terrace,
mirror of the sun and moon,
beneath Kirk Tower of Duddingston.
Chalicing the streams and hidden springs
a sanctuary place invites your offering
swords cast in the lake, bread on the waters.
Each season brings you back
to contemplate what changes
yet continues as before.
Leave something of yourself,
go on to close the circle
by Wells o Wearie beneath St Leonard's Bank,
you reach again to Holyrood's surprise
a Scottish Parliament uprisen.
Gateway for those returning from the hill,
completes a Royal Mile in civic stone.
The crested roofs look out to sea
or fix a watchful eye towards the castle.
From the rectangular back border
forms splay and curve in each direction
wrapping Queensberry House around

where landed dynasts hatched the union.
Then granite blocks mass upward
bearing the debating chamber in their thrust,
an oaken pageant beamed with light.
Above this ensemble still the line
of Calton Hill, democracy's cairns and columns
memorialise war and peace.
This is the lowest point of ground
founded in springs and streams
the building leans towards land and sea
islands of the firth and beacon heights
beneath the shifting lightful sky,
air earth water fire assemble
a Scottish gathering, place and folk
in common purpose, the chorale
to lift our voices to the hill.

Photographs on pages 9, 29, 59, 110 and 118–9 courtesy of Alaisdair Smith (Commissioned by NVA as part of Speed of Light).

Photographs on pages 16, 24, 40, 76, 80, 82, 90, 96 and 104 courtesy of Stuart McHardy.

Photographs on pages 12–13, 50, 55 and 68–9 courtesy of Tom Bee.

Share, explore, experience and celebrate our storytelling heritage.

0131 556 9579

The **Scottish Storytelling Centre** is the home of Scotland's stories on Edinburgh's picturesque Royal Mile. The Centre presents a seasonal programme of storytelling, theatre, dance, music and literature, supported by exciting visual arts, craft and multimedia exhibitions. The Centre also hosts the **Scottish International Storytelling Festival** in October, which is a highlight of Scotland's autumn.

You've seen the landscape, vibrant cities and historic buildings, now experience the magic of live stories and feed your imagination. Don't miss out on the warmth and energy of modern culture inspired by tradition!

Established in 1992, NVA is a registered Scottish arts charity funded by Creative Scotland and a number of UK trusts and foundations. The organisation has produced award winning and dynamic projects in challenging landscapes – these have included temporary lighting animations on the mountains of Skye; permanent spaces such as the Hidden Gardens in Glasgow and major urban festivals.

www.nva.org.uk

LUATH books published in association with NVA

To Have and To Hold: Future of a Contested Landscape

Edited by Gerrie Van Noord for NVA
ISBN 978-1-908373-10-6 PBK £15

Almost 30 years have passed since St Peter's Seminary, designed by Gillespie, Kidd & Coia and noted as Scotland's greatest modernist building, lost its function and was left to the elements.

For the past two and a half years, Glasgow-based public art charity NVA have been working with a number of partners to develop a radical plan for the former seminary and the surrounding woodland. This book brings together a discursive set of texts and raises questions about how we deal with history and heritage, conservation and preservation, owner-ship and decision making around contested sites in the 21st century.

The book is attractive and often fascinating …and a laudable attempt to put a theoretical, philosophical and aesthetic argument for NVA's winning proposal to stabilise the ruin and bring back into artistic use those parts where such an outcome is feasible without vast expense.
THE HERALD

The Storr: Unfolding Landscape

Angus Farquar
ISBN 978-1-905222-22-3 PBK £15

In 2000, the NVA arts organisation created The Path: a night-time walk through Perthshire's Glen Lyon where music, light and international per-formances created an intense sense of pilgrimage that aimed to enhance the participants' sense of the power of the natural landscape and redis-cover what we may have forgotten about the world around us.

This unforgettable event was repeated on one of Europe's most hauntingly beauti-ful landscapes – the high cliffs of Coire Faion and The Storr on Skye. Around midnight, groups equipped with head torches and walking sticks, were guided through this inspiring landscape as the words of Skye's legendary poet Sorley MacLean echoed down from the moun-tain. This book of essays and photo-graphs captures one of the greatest single site-specific environmental art-works ever to be staged in Britain.

This companion records, contextualises and continues an ambitious project, bringing a variety of perspectives to bear. Geology, history, ecology, poetry: all play their part in creating the landscape and the way to construct it for ourselves as something beautiful, something moving.
THE SCOTSMAN

Some other books published by **LUATH** PRESS

A Long Stride Shortens the Road

Donald Smith

ISBN 978-1-842820-73-5 PBK £8.99

A Long Stride Shortens the Road *is a book of poetry that manages to be both intensely Scottish and optimistic.*

THE SCOTSMAN

Donald Smith's is a voice we need to hear in Scotland. He has a story to tell, a vision to shape, a song to declare. Donald writes poetry to say something. His deep knowledge of history, myth, story, religion, landscape and literature means that he has much real richness to draw on.

TESSA RANSFORD

The poems in this collection chart the main staging posts in Scotland's recent history. As writer, theatre director, storyteller and political foot-soldier, Donald Smith has been at the centre of the cultural action. The poems, however, also reveal a personal narrative of exile and attachment, an intimate engagement with Scottish landscape, and a sense of the spiritual in all things.

The Quest for Arthur

Stuart McHardy

ISBN 978-1-842820-12-4 HBK £16.99

King Arthur of Camelot and the Knights of the Round Table are enduring romantic figures.
A national hero for the Britons, the Welsh and the English alike, Arthur is a potent figure for many.

Historian, storyteller and folklorist Stuart McHardy believes he has uncovered the origins of the true Arthur. He incorporates knowledge of folklore and place-name studies with an archaeological understanding of the sixth century.

This quest leads to the discovery that the enigmatic origins of Arthur lie not in Brittany, England or Wales. Instead they lie in that magic land the ancient Welsh called Y Gogledd, 'The North', the North of Britain, which we now call – Scotland.

[Stuart McHardy's] findings are set to shake established Arthurian thinking.

THE SCOTSMAN

Between Ourselves

Donald Smith
ISBN 978-1-906307-92-9 PBK £8.99

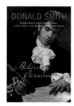

Amongst the dirt and smoke of 18th century Edinburgh, Robert Burns ponders his next move. Frustrated with the Edinburgh literati and the tight purse of his publisher, Burns finds distraction in the capital's dark underbelly. Midnight assignations with working girls and bawdy rhymes for his tavern friends are interrupted when he is unexpectedly called to a mysterious meeting with a dangerous man. But then Burns falls in love, perhaps the only real love in a lifetime of casual romances, with beautiful Nancy, the inspiration for 'Ae Fond Kiss'.

Donald Smith has written the real life love affair of Nancy and Burns into a tantalising tale of passion and betrayal, binding historical fact and fiction together to create an intimate portrait of Burns the man.

The English Spy

Donald Smith
ISBN 978-1-905222-82-7 PBK £8.99

He was a spy among us, but not known as such, otherwise the mob of Edinburgh would pull him to pieces.
JOHN CLERK of Penicuik

Union between England and Scotland hangs in the balance. Propagandist, spy and novelist-to-be Daniel Defoe is caught up in the murky essence of 18th-century Edinburgh – cobblestones, courtesans and kirkyards. Expecting a godly society in the capital of Presbyterianism, Defoe engages with a beautiful Jacobite agent, and uncovers a nest of vipers.

Subtly crafted... and a rattling good yarn.
STEWART CONN

Delves into the City of Literature, and comes out dark side up.
MARC LAMBERT

Excellent...a brisk narrative and a vivid sense of time and place.
THE HERALD

Scotland the Brave Land: 10,000 Years of Scotland in Story

Stuart McHardy
ISBN 978-1-908373-46-6 PBK £7.99

In Scotland there is not a stream or a rock that does not have its story.
STUART MCHARDY

With the release of Disney–Pixar's *Brave*, the world's attention has been drawn to Scotland and its fascinating history. But *Brave* merely scrapes the surface of Scotland's rich storytelling culture. This collection of tales is the next step for anyone wishing to look further into the traditions of Scotland. These enchanting tales reflect the wide diversity of its heritage and there are few aspects of Scottish tradition that have escaped memorialisation in folklore.

With its captivation, and often gruesome, tales of heroic warriors in battle, bold heroines, deceitful aristocracy, and supernatural creatures, *Scotland the Brave Land* is a journey into the cultural heritage and a glimpse at the folklore carried through oral tradition for more than 10,000 years.

Tales of Bonnie Prince Charlie and the Jacobites

Stuart McHardy
ISBN 978-1-908373-23-6 PBK £7.99

Great battles, great characters and great stories underpin our understanding of the Jacobite period; one of the most romanticised eras in Scottish history.

From the exploits of charismatic Bonnie Prince Charlie to the many ingenious ways the Jacobites outwitted the Redcoats, Stuart McHardy has gathered together some of the best tales from the period.

Find out the best way to escape from Edinburgh Castle and where to look for Prince Charlie's enchanted gold. Discover the story behind one Highlander who swapped his kilt for a dress, and more, in this salute to the ancient Scots tradition of storytelling.

A New History of the Picts

Stuart McHardy

ISBN 978-1-906817-70-1 PBK £8.99

The Picts hold a special place in the Scottish mindset – a mysterious race of painted warriors, leaving behind imposing standing stones and not much more. Stuart McHardy challenges these long-held historical assumptions. He aims to get to the truth of who the Picts really were, and what their influence has been on Scotland's past and present.

McHardy demonstrates that rather than being some historical group of outsiders, or mysterious invaders, the Picts were in fact the indigenous people of Scotland and the most significant of our tribal ancestors. The Picts were not wiped out in battle, but gradually integrated with the Scots to form Alba. Their descendants walk our streets today.

Written and arranged in a way that is both accessible and scholarly, this is an excellent addition to the growing body of work on the Picts.

THE COURIER

Pagan Symbols of the Picts

Stuart McHardy

ISBN 978-1-908373-14-4 HBK £14.99

The Pagan Symbols of the Picts offers a fresh perspective on the importance of art, symbolism and the Picts in Scotland's cultural history. By looking beyond historical written accounts from Roman, Irish and Northumbrian sources, Stuart McHardy challenges traditional interpretations of Pictish stone art. Neither commemorative monuments nor an early alphabet, he instead explores their binary existence; as examples of larger shared beliefs in a linguistically and politically diverse landscape, and as objects of a very local genesis and influence. *The Pagan Symbols of the Picts* reveals not only the significance of Pictish symbology in the course of everyday life, but its place in the larger history of the Picts in Scotland and beyond.

Examining the temporal and geographic, the cultural and mythical, the artistic and oral, Stuart McHardy paints a vivid and diverse picture of Pictish Scotland.

Details of these and other books published by Luath Press can be found at:
www.luath.co.uk

Luath Press Limited
committed to publishing well written books worth reading

LUATH PRESS takes its name from Robert Burns, whose little collie Luath (*Gael.,* swift or nimble) tripped up Jean Armour at a wedding and gave him the chance to speak to the woman who was to be his wife and the abiding love of his life. Burns called one of 'The Twa Dogs' Luath after Cuchullin's hunting dog in Ossian's *Fingal*. Luath Press was established in 1981 in the heart of Burns country, and is now based a few steps up the road from Burns' first lodgings on Edinburgh's Royal Mile.

Luath offers you distinctive writing with a hint of unexpected pleasures.

Most bookshops in the UK, the US, Canada, Australia, New Zealand and parts of Europe either carry our books in stock or can order them for you. To order direct from us, please send a £sterling cheque, postal order, international money order or your credit card details (number, address of cardholder and expiry date) to us at the address below. Please add post and packing as follows: UK – £1.00 per delivery address; overseas surface mail – £2.50 per delivery address; overseas airmail – £3.50 for the first book to each delivery address, plus £1.00 for each additional book by airmail to the same address. If your order is a gift, we will happily enclose your card or message at no extra charge.

Luath Press Limited
543/2 Castlehill
The Royal Mile
Edinburgh EH1 2ND
Scotland
Telephone: 0131 225 4326 (24 hours)
Fax: 0131 225 4324
email: sales@luath.co.uk
Website: www.luath.co.uk